Beyond the Cross

Embracing God's grace for broken believers

Rich Beeler

with Wesley Shropshire

WestBow
PRESS
A DIVISION OF THOMAS NELSON

WestBow Press books may be ordered through booksellers or by contacting:

WestBow Press
A Division of Thomas Nelson
1663 Liberty Drive
Bloomington, IN 47403
www.westbowpress.com
1-(866) 928-1240

ISBN : 978-1-4497-2880-9 (sc)
ISBN: 978-1-4497-2881-6 (hc)
ISBN: 978-1-4497-2879-3 (e)

Library of Congress Control Number: 2011918469

Printed in the United States of America

WestBow Press rev. date: 11/11/2011

For my college students:
You are the reason God wakes
me up every morning.

No one has ever out-sinned me, but I can never out-sin grace.

—*Rich Beeler, 2007*

Contents

Preface   ix
Introduction   xi
Chapter 1   Favored Sons   3
Chapter 2   The Blindside   12
Chapter 3   The Great Giveaway   23
Chapter 4   Slipping into Darkness   33
Chapter 5   Eating with Pigs   42
Chapter 6   Sinking to Rise No More   50
Chapter 7   Hand of God   63
Chapter 8   One Small Step   74
Chapter 9   The Other Side of Grace   85
Chapter 10   Silencing the Accuser   96
Chapter 11   The Great Exchange   109
Chapter 12   Born Again   119
Chapter 13   Embracing the Wreckage   131
Chapter 14   No Day but Today   141
Epilogue   151
Notes   155

Preface

Far too many Christians are deceived into thinking that coming to the cross is a one-time event. They believe that once they have been there and had their past sins wiped away, the rest is up to them; that any future grace they might enjoy is contingent solely upon their performance as faithful servants of Christ, and should they fail in their performance, they are disqualified from their servanthood. This flawed thinking assumes that when one who should know better experiences moral failure, he or she is no longer of value to the kingdom of God. Grace is seen as something that God extends only to unsaved sinners seeking salvation.

Nothing could be further from the truth. Many Christians in our culture have committed their most heinous sins and experienced their biggest spiritual failures after coming to Christ. And some of them remain hopelessly paralyzed by the perceived reality that God's redeeming grace is no longer available to them.

Beyond the Cross is not a book about leaving the cross of Jesus Christ behind. It is about rediscovering its constant shadow. It is about giving hope to broken believers that God's grace is just as available and powerful to them as it is to unredeemed sinners coming to the cross for the very first time. God really does rescue and restore His own! Grace cascades from Calvary's mount in all directions, springing forth for sinners seeking redemption and for Christians seeking restoration. Embracing the precious cross of Jesus Christ is definitely not a one-time event.

It is a lifelong journey.

Introduction

It was the last day of the month. The idea of writing a book had been swirling through my brain for weeks, but lately, it had begun to feel more like an obsession. I could sense the Holy Spirit speaking to me about chapter titles, Bible verses, and pieces of my life story that I needed to share. But the questions were there as well.

Was I really supposed to do this? Was this God or just some concoction of my imagination? I had never written a book, let alone one about a subject as incomprehensible as the grace of God. Besides, who was I to think people would want to hear my story? I was desperate for God to give me direction. So I began to beg Him for it. Like I said, it was the last day of the month.

A few weeks earlier, I had started a quiet-time ritual of reading and meditating on one Psalm each day. My plan was to do thirty a month for five months. I must say, God had been doing some pretty incredible things in my life as a result of these times of spiritual meditation. But now, I was depending on Him to speak loudly and clearly. Was I supposed to write this book or not? I became convinced that the answer was in the Psalms.

It was the last day of February, so the plan called for me to read two extra Psalms that day to get to my monthly quota of thirty. I came home from work, slipped into my comfortable clothes, and went to my secret place where I meet with God every day. I prayed, asking the Lord to give me clear direction about this book idea from His Word. Then I began to read Psalms 28, 29, and 30.

As only the Psalms can do, their lofty poetic language took my spirit to places where only angels dare to tread. Chapters 28 and 29 were powerful declarations of the glory and majesty of God. I heard many things in my spirit, but none that seemed to pertain to the book. Then I turned the page to Psalm 30. And there before me, on the pages of God's Holy Word, was my life story.

> I will exalt you, Lord, for you lifted me out of the depths and did not let my enemies gloat over me.
>
> Lord my God, I called to you for help, and you healed me.
>
> You, Lord, brought me up from the realm of the dead; you spared me from going down to the pit.
>
> Sing the praises of the Lord, you his faithful people; praise his holy name!
>
> For his anger lasts only a moment, but his favor lasts a lifetime; weeping may stay for the night, but rejoicing comes in the morning.
>
> When I felt secure, I said, 'I will never be shaken.'
>
> Lord, when you favored me, you made my royal mountain stand firm; but when you hid your face, I was dismayed.
>
> To you, Lord, I called; to the Lord I cried for mercy:
>
> "What is gained if I am silenced, if I go down to the pit? Will the dust praise you? Will it proclaim your faithfulness?

Hear, Lord, and be merciful to me; Lord, be my help."

You turned my wailing into dancing; you removed my sackcloth and clothed me with joy,

That my heart may sing your praises and not be silent. Lord my God, I will praise you forever (Psalm 30).

That was my story! Down to the last word, it was a poetic chronicle of my journey as a Christian. I had begun as a son of the King of Kings, highly favored and used mightily in the kingdom. At the age of twenty-seven, I had everything a young Christian man could possibly have going for him. What followed was an inexplicable and devastating five-year detour from my walk with God marked by spiritual rebellion and self-destructive behavior. That dark passage and the subsequent rescue of grace that I experienced is outlined almost verbatim by David's amazing story in Psalm 30. But what is even more amazing is that it isn't just my story. It is Wesley's story, too.

Wesley Shropshire is a man more than twenty years younger than me, whom I had helped disciple when he was a teenager. When he became a young adult, I was able to mentor Wes as my true son in the faith, just as Timothy was to Paul. In between were five of the most difficult years of my life and his, when Wes took an inexplicable and devastating detour from his walk with God. His path from the ages of eighteen to twenty-three was a dark passage marked by rebellion against God and a pattern of blatantly self-destructive behavior.

The parallels are staggering. And though our wayward journeys took place almost exactly a decade apart in life, both Wes and I know that our stories are powerfully interconnected. And they are not unique.

The process we have been through is one faced by all too many Christians in our culture today. Our churches are filled with men and women who began their journeys of faith with the promise of doing great things for the name of Christ only to have their Christian existence ambushed by a vicious and unforeseen onslaught of the Enemy. The struggle can be suffocating; the failure disheartening; the guilt debilitating.

We did not write this book from a perspective of theology or theory. Nor is it a made-up story. It is as raw and as candid as we could possibly write it, offering hope to the person reading this right now who cannot imagine how God could ever forgive them, not to mention use them again. This is for people with real train wrecks in their lives.

This book is for those precious sons and daughters of God who have seen their dreams turn to nightmares. This book is for the college-age believer who can't even get on the computer to write a paper without being sucked into a whirlpool of pornography. It is for the single Christian girl who can't imagine how she's going to tell her parents she's having a baby, let alone that she doesn't know for sure who the father is. It is for the young adult believer who can't get a job because of the drug charges on his record. This is for the Christian guy who has lost count of how many girls he's slept with in the past year, and who prays every night that one of them isn't pregnant. In the wake of such carnage, the question is always the same: Does God really extend grace and restoration to people who are already redeemed and who should have known better?

As Wes and I share our stories, we hope to do so from the perspective of two Christ-followers who have wrestled with that same question. It is one thing for a lost person to make a mess of his life—no one doubts that God's mercy is abundant toward those who do so ignorantly in unbelief. But the truth we have painfully experienced is that many Christians make the same kinds of messes—sometimes even bigger ones. That is why we are compelled to tell our stories and to proclaim the glorious truth we have come to embrace. There is a fountain of grace for all who would come to the cross.

Even those who have been there before.

Rich Beeler
Corryton, Tennessee
March 2011

Section One: The Slippery Slope

"But each one is tempted when he is drawn away by his own desires and enticed. Then, when desire has conceived, it gives birth to sin; and sin, when it is full-grown, brings forth death. Do not be deceived, my beloved brethren" (James 1:14-16 NKJV).

Chapter 1

Favored Sons

> "Behold, what manner of love the Father hath bestowed upon us, that we should be called the sons of God" (1 John 3:1 KJV).

A good start does not guarantee a good finish. But it certainly helps. Even the most casual observers of Christian behavior would agree that most believers get off to a pretty good start in the faith. The Bible is filled with stories of heroes who began their journeys with God and quickly became spirit-filled warriors of the kingdom. For many of these believers, the early years of their faith produced a continuing upward curve on the graph of spiritual growth. Such was true for the beginning of Rich Beeler's journey.

Rich: I was saved at the age of nine, in a revival meeting at a little country church in east Tennessee. I didn't know all there was to know about theology, only that I was a sinner who needed a Savior. I remember like it was yesterday, praying to receive Christ after the service in the pastor's office with my mom by my side. It seemed such a natural part of the process for one who had grown up in a family as loving and nurturing as mine. As I grew into my teenage years, my life as a believer was fairly typical. I knew I was a Christian, but the spiritual aspect of my life was generally kept neatly in its Sunday compartment. That began to change during my junior year of high school. I started attending different churches in the community and was really challenged in my faith, listening to some dynamic young pastors. I developed a passion for seeing my friends come to know Jesus. My senior year, I led a buddy to Christ who had never heard the gospel. He would later become a missionary to the Ukraine, leading people half a world away to saving faith.

The passion of a new Christian can be truly contagious. As 2 Corinthians 5:17 (NKJV) says, "All things have become new." The desire to glorify God with your life consumes your thought processes. It isn't particularly hard to witness or share your faith. You can't help but tell people how great God is, what He has done for you, and what He wants to do for them. Sharing the gospel just seems to come naturally. This newness of life in Christ can be especially exciting for a high school student. Wes Shropshire was just such a student.

Wes: I came to Christ and was baptized as a sophomore in high school. My student pastor, CH Qualls, had been a powerful influence on me during middle school. He had not only been a strong Christian role model, but he had shown me the love of Christ in a way I had never known it. I had grown up in a home that was filled with violence and drug abuse and had never really been exposed to spiritual truth. I was blown away by this college-aged guy who could love a kid with my background unconditionally and show me how Christ would do the same. Being a high school student at my church was amazing. I was surrounded by a solid group of friends who helped steer my life in a positive direction. I couldn't really see any good that would come from hanging out with the "party kids," and my friends at church really reinforced that belief. When my best friend Chad became a believer after our sophomore year, I felt like I finally had the strong brother I needed to walk alongside me.

Unlimited potential

There is something uniquely powerful about being young and in the will of God. When your whole life is ahead of you and you're walking with God, you feel as if there is literally no limit to what you can accomplish as His servant. Both Wes and Rich envisioned a life characterized by strong marriages, godly children, and effective service in the kingdom of God. They didn't know all the details, but they knew God had a plan for their lives.

King David knew the same thing. And he knew it long before he became king. The shepherd boy of Bethlehem received the call of God to rule His people some fifteen years before assuming the throne, probably around the age of fifteen or sixteen. And talk about getting off to a good start! Shortly after receiving his anointing for the destiny God had scheduled for him, David conquered the enemy that had the whole Israeli army paralyzed with fear, becoming a national hero overnight. David must have thought that the potential for his spiritual future was unlimited.

This is actually quite typical of most young Christ-followers who have experienced good beginnings to their spiritual journeys. Being part of a dynamic fellowship of believers, which Wes and Rich both had with their church, really has no substitute in preparing a young Christian for the life God made him to live. When a believer is surrounded by a strong spiritual family and is regularly being fed from the Word, it is hard for him not to think God has incredible plans for his life.

Rich: My faith had really begun to grow during my senior year in high school. I was genuinely concerned about my friends coming to know Christ. There were inklings in my spirit that God might have a special purpose for my life, and it was on a Sunday night at Fairview Baptist Church when that inkling became a calling. I was sitting with my best friend, Kevin, listening to the pastor. I don't remember his message that night, but I do remember God's. His Spirit spoke clearly to mine, "I want you to do what that man up there behind that pulpit is doing." (Huh? Are you talking to me, God, or am I just overhearing your conversation with Kevin?) I was terrified. So much so that I didn't answer for almost three more years. But I couldn't deny the call. I knew His voice.

Most Christians receive their callings at a young age. In fact, some surveys have indicated that the average missionary senses the call to missions by age eleven. But whether we are called to the mission field, the pulpit, or some other full-time Christian service, the call of God is evident to anyone who walks closely with Him. This can be especially true during the early years of the journey. And a call can involve more things than might meet the eye.

Some people have sensed the call to be adoptive parents. Others may feel God's Spirit moving them to some field or profession that sounds secular, such as education, law, or medicine. The truth is, to a true follower of Christ, nothing is secular. As 2 Corinthians 5:18 says, "All things are of God." When we walk with Him, He will speak to our heart about the destiny He has for us. For Rich, that involved preaching. For others, it involves career and family. For Wesley, it involved changing the course of his entire history.

Wes: I did not grow up in a Christian home. My parents had split up when I was about six years old, so I could barely remember what it was like to be raised in a two-parent home. I lived with my mom until I was in the sixth grade. I had two different step-dads in four years. One was a mean drunk. Some nights, he would come home and beat my mom so bad she would have to go to the hospital. This scenario often left me and my two brothers home alone. Eventually, it became apparent to our family that we could no longer stay in this situation. When I was twelve, we went to live with our dad. My mom, whom I had never been separated from until that point, was never part of my life again. I know these experiences left emotional scars on me, but after I came to Christ, I could sense God calling me to change the direction of my family history. I was determined to someday have a godly marriage that stayed together and honored Christ above all.

As Bible heroes go, the subject of unlimited potential not only applies to David. It brings Saul to mind as well. Israel's first king was selected not so much for his hidden spiritual qualities, but rather he was just the obvious choice. Standing over seven feet tall, the Bible describes Saul as a strong, handsome warrior who certainly would have stood out in a crowd. He led the armies of Israel to numerous victories over their enemies and was immensely popular with the people.

Ironically, it was Saul's victories that turned out to be his undoing. Rather than remain humbly obedient to God, Saul became arrogant and careless in the aftermath of battle. Once he built a statue in his own honor rather than giving glory and credit to the Lord. On another occasion, he even performed the duties of the high priest in his impatience to make sacrifices. It was this arrogance that ultimately caused God to rip the kingdom from Saul's hands.

As far as the Bible tells us, the only people who knew that God was in the process of removing Saul from power were Saul himself and the prophet Samuel. The people were oblivious. Anyone would have been. Everything about Saul looked strong and victorious on the surface. His armies were winning victories, and the kingdom was growing. God was using him. What could possibly be wrong?

Kingdom servants

When a Christian is on the verge of taking a spiritual fall, seldom is it evident from the outside. Often what is known about us by fellow believers has to do with that which is visible and apparent. Are we showing up at church? Are we still leading the Bible study? Do we still smile and tell people we're praying for them? Does God seem to be using us? Those are the surefire signs of a Christian who has it together. Aren't they?

Rich: I was twenty-five years old when one of the deacons at church approached me after a service. "You know, we just had an election to choose five new deacons," he said. "You're one of the five." I didn't know what to say. I knew what a premium my church placed on spiritual leadership and being selected as a deacon was no small matter, especially for a twenty-five-year-old. I went through a rigorous approval process and was ultimately chosen by the deacon board to serve. It remains to this day one of the most truly humbling experiences of my life. The following year, I was elected vice-chair. Our pastor, Dr. Rocky Ramsey, had allowed me to fill the pulpit in his absence on several occasions to help develop my preaching gift. Rocky was a gifted communicator who did not take lightly the issue of teaching God's Word. His confidence in me was an incredible affirmation as a young preacher. I really felt as though God was preparing me for something significant.

Peter surely felt the same thing. Jesus had poured three years of His life into him and the other eleven disciples. The wisdom they had gained and the profound teaching and spectacular miracles they had heard and experienced firsthand had to be preparing them for something immensely significant. They were going to be used in a mighty way. And they were ready. At least, Peter knew that he was.

"Lord, I am ready to go with you to prison and to death," he told Jesus one night.

"I tell you the truth, Peter," Jesus replied. "Before the rooster crows today, you will deny three times that you know me" (Luke 22:33-34).

"Not me, Lord! Haven't you been paying attention? Am I not the guy that's always out front, leading the charge to do all this stuff you've been teaching us? Oh no, not me, Jesus. I'm with you to the end."

Nearly all of us have thought something like that at one time or another. When we are already serving God at a level beyond what we ever expected, our zeal toward the future is powerful. Even if that future is unknown. There is something especially exciting about as yet unrealized potential. There seem to be literally no boundaries to what God can accomplish through our lives. The sky really is the limit.

Wes: During the last half of my senior year in high school, Chad and I got a really strong burden for one of our friends and soccer teammates. Dane was the most popular guy on campus, the quarterback for the football team. You might say he was Mr. Personality. But what few people realized was that there was a huge void in his life that we knew only Christ could fill. We began to pray regularly for him and invite him to church or just to hang out. That spring, Chris Tomlin did a concert at our church and during the music, Dane just broke down. He was sitting between Chad and me, and it seemed like all the sin and brokenness of his life just spilled out there on the floor. After graduation, Dane, the most popular party guy in the school, skipped his senior trip and went to church camp with Chad and me. On the last night of camp, Dane broke down again in front of the whole leadership team. "I never knew people could love me like that," he said. I was as blown away as he was. I never knew God could use me like that.

Like Wes and Rich, many Christians can recall a time in their life when God used them more powerfully than they thought He ever could. You may recall just such a time in your own life, a time when the power of God was so evident in you that you just couldn't wait for the next opportunity to see Him move. Those times may seem like a distant memory from a place so far away that you can never go there again.

Peter had heard the noise thousands of times before. But it had never sounded like this. He remembered many conversations with Jesus; the in-depth subjects they had discussed by late-night campfires were endless. He had dreamed of some of those talks that night, though sleep did not come easily. A few hours earlier, he was certain an incredible God-ordained destiny was in his immediate future. Now he had no idea what the future might hold. Only that everything felt wrong.

"Maybe it was all a dream," he thought to himself. He had been awakened with a start by that all-too-familiar sound. Perhaps he had imagined it. The mind can play tricks, especially when sleep is involved. He lay there in dead silence as the minutes seemed like hours. Suddenly his dark solitude was shattered.

As a rooster crowed again.

Questions to consider:

A good start does not guarantee a good finish. Are you building the necessary elements into your walk of faith to be able to finish your Christian life well?

The Bible tells us that spiritual pride is extremely dangerous. Are you humbly trusting the Holy Spirit to keep you pure and obedient in your walk?

Truth to embrace:

The Christian life is not a sprint; it is a marathon.

"You need to persevere so that when you have done the will of God, you will receive what he has promised" (Hebrews 10:36).

But for the grace of God, we are all capable of falling.

"Pride goes before destruction, a haughty spirit before a fall" (Proverbs 16:18).

We must humbly trust God to keep us on the right path.

"To him who is able to keep you from stumbling and to present you before his glorious presence without fault and with great joy" (Jude 24).

Chapter 2

The Blindside

> "Therefore let him who thinks he stands take heed lest he fall"
> (1 Corinthians 10:12 NKJV).

No person successfully engaged in the Christian life thinks he is going to fall. It just doesn't happen to people like us. Spiritual and moral failure happens to people of poor integrity, like televangelists. We assume they're really just out for money, so it's a matter of time before they mess up morally. But failure doesn't happen to people who are serving God with a clear conscience. Right?

It would never happen to a man like King David. Everyone was sure of that. The people of Israel could not have asked for a leader with purer motives or godlier intentions. Before God gave David the kingdom, He even referred to him as "a man after my own heart."

What a thing to have said about you! It just doesn't get any better than that. We've all had compliments thrown at us and encouraging things said to us. But to have the Lord of heaven and earth call someone a man after His own heart pretty well ensures that that person is never going to stray from the paths of righteousness. Or so you would think.

Dropping your guard

No one is invulnerable to moral failure. In fact, the Bible gives a stern warning in Paul's first letter to the Corinthians that the person most vulnerable to such failure is the one who thinks he is not.

"So, if you think you are standing firm, be careful that you don't fall!" (1 Corinthians 10:12).

But what would make someone think such a thing? The Bible, as well as our own life experience, tells us that anyone can mess up. Yet many Christians lack the one precious ingredient in their lives that is our greatest protection against moral catastrophe: accountability.

Rich: I never drank, took drugs, or had premarital sex as a teenager. In fact, I was absolutely certain I would never do any of those things. It broke my heart when my friends indulged in them during high school and college. "If only they had my moral fortitude. I would never do that" was my attitude. I had great moral intentions. But I had little or no accountability. I was involved in the youth ministry at our church, and most of my spiritual energy was spent discipling high school kids. I never attended a community group with people my own age. My closest brothers in Christ were teenagers. I had an obligation to prepare lessons and Bible study materials. But I had no one in my life to really challenge me spiritually. This scenario caused me to develop a great sense of spiritual security. And it was a false one.

What Rich was unable to see was slowly developing into a very dangerous blind spot in his spiritual life. A great many Christians have these same blind spots and don't even know it. One of the inherent dangers of serving God effectively is that it takes great focus. And focus often creates blind spots.

Blind spots are areas of our lives that we unwittingly stop paying attention to. And they can be vital areas. Our needs for significance, security, and intimacy can often end up in these black holes. And that isn't all that ends up there. The Enemy loves to creep into our blind spots and just wait for the opportune time to strike. Without strong accountability partners in our lives, we will never see him coming.

One of the Enemy's primary strategies is to isolate us. Ecclesiastes 4 talks about the importance of fellowship and the incredible strength of a threefold cord.

"Though one may be overpowered, two can defend themselves. A cord of three strands is not quickly broken" (Ecclesiastes 4:12).

Wes, Chad, and Dane knew that kind of strength. But with the onset of college, the strands began to unravel. And Wes was the first to experience the fallout of the isolation.

Wes: The summer after my graduation was great. It seemed like Dane, Chad, and I grew closer every day. We really fed off each other spiritually. I think we felt like we could take on the world. But we never thought about the fact that it was all so temporary. In the fall, Chad and Dane both moved away to school, and suddenly, I was left alone. I still had my relationship with Christ, but without my closest brothers, I was more vulnerable than I could have possibly realized. There was no one in my life to hold me accountable, and the constant spiritual feeding I had experienced in the youth group was not there either. I can't completely explain the turn my life took, but looking back now, I can see how I was a sitting duck.

David could relate. The day he became king of the nation of Israel should have been the greatest day of his life. After all, it was his God-given destiny. But David could scarcely bring himself to celebrate. His ascension to the throne had been precipitated by the death of King Saul in battle, who had once been a mentor and surrogate father to David. And alongside Saul, lying dead on the battlefield, was David's best friend and spiritual brother Jonathan.

During their youth, David and Jonathan had a relationship that had tremendously sharpened both men in their walks with God. They were there for each other; they prayed for each other; they encouraged each other; they held each other accountable. It is no mystery or coincidence that David's life during that time was characterized by one wise spiritual decision after another. But now Jonathan was gone. And as David would eventually realize, so was his accountability—a scenario that would lead the king down paths he never thought he would take.

Initial assault

David survived without Jonathan. For a while. He continued to govern the country and win great military victories. He had sons and daughters and was beloved by an entire nation. He loved many women. But he never found another Jonathan. What he did find were a group of advisors who were really good at one thing: telling the king exactly what he wanted to hear.

No one was there to challenge and sharpen David. And As any of us might, the king gradually became dull and lazy. One spring, he even decided to stay home while his armies went off to war. To the average citizen of Judea, this was not a big deal. The king surely knew what he was doing, and besides if anybody deserved a little vacation, it was David. But Jonathan would have sensed that something was very wrong. This was not like David at all. Neither were evening strolls on the roof.

Rich: I remember the conversation vividly. My youth pastor, Butch Parker, asked me a question that I thought was strange. "Who challenges you spiritually?" I had never heard anyone ask such a thing, and I had no clue how to answer. Butch observed that I spent a lot of time ministering to high school students as a youth worker, but he suggested that I needed someone closer to my own peer group to help sharpen me. I wasn't sure how to react. Did something like that even matter? We didn't really have a college ministry at the time. Besides, I challenged myself spiritually. And it didn't bother me a bit that I was spiritually more mature than most of the people around me. Yet a few weeks later, I couldn't get the conversation off my mind. Was I in danger? It's difficult to explain, but I began to sense a presence of evil lurking close to my life that I couldn't identify. And it was becoming almost oppressive. I shared this with one of the senior guys one Sunday night after church, but neither of us could make sense of it. I didn't realize it then, but the Enemy was in my blind spot. That night, I rented my first pornographic video.

As out of character as this poor moral choice may have been for Rich, it was no more so than the choice King David was about to make as he walked along the roof of the palace that evening. He was a man after God's own heart. He loved the Lord and wanted to obey Him. His intentions were noble. But as the often quoted proverb goes, "the road to hell is paved with good intentions."

This wise saying reminds us that even the best intentions provide no guarantee that we will make the right choices. David's direction was bad, and no one was there to point it out. There was no Jonathan in his life to remind him that lying around the palace, staying up late, and sleeping till noon was not behavior fit for the king. The lack of accountability and true spiritual intimacy in David's life was about to play out in a sordid series of events that would remind Bible students forever of a timeless truth: The best of us is capable of the worst in us.

And more often than not, the worst is worse than we can imagine.

Wes: During the fall after my high school graduation, I suddenly found myself on my own spiritually. At least that's how it felt. Chad and Dane were away at school, and I ended up moving in with some guys who weren't following Christ. I thought I could handle myself, but I just failed to recognize that there were huge blind spots in my life. Before I knew it, I had slipped right into secular collegiate culture. It wasn't long until I had let alcohol into my life. Without the spiritual intimacy I got from my friendship with my brothers in Christ, I unconsciously started seeking it in other people and places. My new relationships were leading me into more and more of a partying lifestyle. Protective spiritual fences began crumbling in my life. Just before Christmas, I did something I thought I would never do: I lost my virginity to a girl who was not my wife. It was devastating. It was like the future I had dreamed of was shattered. I told Rich I felt like a piece of me was gone, and I could never get it back.

From the roof of the palace, most of the city lay in a downhill direction so many of the nearby courtyards were easily visible. Outside a neighboring house, David saw a woman bathing. He knew he should look away, but she was so beautiful. And he felt so alone. He just wanted to feel close to someone. Maybe the woman was alone as well. He could always ask. After all, he was the king. And no one was there to tell him no.

"David sent someone to find out about her. The man said, 'She is Bathsheba, the daughter of Eliam and the wife of Uriah the Hittite.' Then David sent messengers to get her. She came to him, and he slept with her." (2 Samuel 11:3-4).

Unending struggle

David's rendezvous of pleasure with Bathsheba may have felt like ecstasy in the dark of night, but it looked a lot like adultery in the light of day. The shame the king felt that next morning was no doubt overwhelming. How could he have been so blind? He would send her home immediately. Neither of them would ever speak of this again. It was a mistake, but it was over.

If only it were that simple.

Rich: I won't lie; there was a feeling of exhilaration when I slipped into the adult room of the video store. I was doing something incredibly forbidden, but I was a grown man, and I could do it without anyone stopping me. Sin tends to feel that way under cover of the night. But the day always comes. The following morning, I felt so ashamed. How could I have been so stupid? What if someone had seen me? How could I commit such an abomination in the eyes of God? I had sinned before, but this just felt so much dirtier. I later learned that what I was feeling was exactly what Paul described in 1 Corinthians 6:18 when he said, "Whoever sins sexually, sins against their own body." I was desperate with guilt. I did the only thing that made sense to me. I got "saved." In the mind of a young man who had never had sex or even drank a beer, this seemed like a sin that was beyond anything a real Christian could do. So in the privacy of a bathroom in my office building, I prayed the sinner's prayer. I went that evening and shared my new "salvation" with our youth pastor. He was a bit stunned as was the rest of the church. But they re-baptized me, and I set off on what I thought was a new journey. I would soon find out that my problems had nothing to do with being lost. And they were still there. This attempt at a quick fix for a much deeper problem was the beginning of a monumental struggle in my life that would rage over the next three years.

It had been nearly two months since David had heard from Bathsheba. Not that he hadn't thought about her. She was stunning. He knew the decision to end their brief affair was right—after all, she was another man's wife. And not just any man. Bathsheba's husband was Uriah the Hittite, one of the most trusted commanders in

David's army. Still, they had shared such an amazing night together. They seemed like soulmates. It felt so right.

"But it was wrong," David reminded himself. "It can't go on. Even with Uriah away on the battlefield, I can't see her again."

This is the struggle that ensues the moment a believer gives any voice to the flesh. The flesh has a ravenous appetite. In fact, every time you feed it, your flesh only comes back hungrier than before. For someone who does not know the Lord, this presents no apparent problem. He simply caters to his desires and gives his flesh what it wants. But for a believer, an unending war begins, pitting his unredeemed flesh in a death match with his spirit, which longs to live for God. It is the fiercest battle a Christian will ever encounter.

Wes: After I messed up sexually, I immediately stopped seeing the girl and ran into the arms of Christ. I was so broken over what I had done that I knew I would never do it again. The pain was just too great. What I didn't realize was that I had awakened the sleeping giant of my flesh. And while my spirit was desperately crying out for repentance and return to the Lord, my flesh and its appetites would never sleep again. As much as I wanted to put the whole thing behind me, the same blind spots that had made me vulnerable to attack were still there in my life. My next dating relationship became sexual as well. One night, Rich confronted me about the way I was living. I broke down in a flood of emotion. The struggle between my flesh and my spirit was killing me. I wanted to live for the Lord, but I just kept failing Him. I told Rich I had broken the relationship off, but I also confessed that sexual temptation was killing me. During the spring, I had slipped back into partying and hanging out with people who were not believers. I told Rich that every time I got a call from a girl I had been with, the temptation was just too great. Jesus told us that sometimes living pure requires drastic measures. I was desperate to be free, so one night, I threw my cell phone in a dumpster and walked away. I wish I could say that was the end of my struggles. But I still had a flesh. I had not thrown that away.

Jesus told His disciples in Mark 14:38, "Pray so that you will not fall into temptation." But why was this avoidance of temptation so important? Because of what Jesus said next: "The spirit is willing, but the flesh is weak" (Mark 14:38).

Each of us knows to one degree or another what it is to desire to follow and obey Christ but to lack the strength to carry out those desires. It is the defining struggle of the Christian life. Paul devoted nearly a whole chapter to it in Romans 7, which is one of the most authentic depictions of this real-life battle found anywhere in Scripture. In Romans 7:19, Paul writes the following description of his own Christian journey:

"For I do not do the good I want to do, but the evil I do not want to do—this I keep on doing" (Romans 7:19).

Such is the struggle of a Christ-follower in this world. And sometimes the fighting can become so relentless that letting go seems to be the only viable option. In Genesis 32, we have the strange account of Jacob wrestling with God in a match that lasted until the breaking of the day. Jacob's victory in this divine encounter would become the defining moment for the man who was destined to become the patriarch of the nation of Israel. But just before the sunrise, God says a most unusual thing to Jacob, "Let me go" (Genesis 32:26).

Now why on earth would the Lord tell one of his beloved sons to let go in a struggle God knows is going to end in victory if the believer just holds on? Because of one tragic reality: most people let go. For many Christians, when the battle gets so heated that they think they can't hold on another moment, they don't. They give up.

Thank God, Jacob held on. Rich and Wes were both determined to do the same. So was David. He was no doubt tormented day and night by both guilt and temptation, but surely he would fight through this, and victory would come. And then the message arrived from Bathsheba. It was brief: "I'm pregnant."

Suddenly, letting go sounded like a viable option.

Questions to consider:

Who challenges you spiritually?

Do you have trusted people in your life who hold you accountable in your walk with Christ?

Truth to embrace:

We need strong brothers and sisters in Christ to help us grow and hold us accountable.

"As iron sharpens iron, so one person sharpens another" (Proverbs 27:17).

There is great power in fellowship with strong believers.

"Though one may be overpowered, two can defend themselves. A cord of three strands is not quickly broken" (Ecclesiastes 4:12).

We must have people in our lives who are willing to go the distance with us.

"And Jonathan made a covenant with David because he loved him as himself. Jonathan took off the robe he was wearing and gave it to David, along with his tunic, and even his sword, his bow and his belt" (1 Samuel 18:3–4).

Chapter 3

The Great Giveaway

> "Therefore God gave them over in the sinful desires of
> their hearts"
> (Romans 1:24).

Lot never imagined things would end up like this. It seemed as though only a few months had passed since he had left his uncle Abraham and set off toward the rich, fertile valley of the Jordan River. His uncle had warned him not to put too much trust in what his eyes told him. But the land looked so inviting. He knew the city of Sodom was no place for a man of God, but he had that all figured out. He and his family would live outside the city gates.

After a while, the inconvenience of transporting wool and hides back and forth from their camp to the city began to weigh on Lot. And he had to admit the nightlife in Sodom was pretty enticing. It really made more sense to just buy a little house inside the gates. Uncle Abraham and his family back in Canaan would no doubt be disappointed in such a compromising move. Abraham had been like a father to Lot since he was just a boy. But his uncle was getting on in years, and he just didn't understand the new ways of the world.

There was so much money to be made, so much of life to experience in a place like Sodom!

Faulty logic

Up to now, Lot had not been able to ignore the whisper deep within his spirit telling him he was somewhere he had no business being. But lately, the voice was being overpowered by the sounds of music, dancing, and celebration emanating from just beyond the city walls. Finally, Lot could take it no more. He gathered his family and their belongings and moved to a house inside the gates of Sodom. Uncle Abraham would just have to understand. Lot was a man now, and this was his decision.

> *Rich: My struggle with pornography continued over the next three years. It was a vicious cycle of temptation, sin, guilt, confession, and a subsequent return to the sin. But as is usually the case when sin patterns develop in our lives, my problems grew beyond the realm of pornography. For the first time in my life, I tried alcohol. The very first night I drank, I got extremely intoxicated. But while the next day brought a sizable hangover, the guilt that accompanied it was nothing like what I experienced with sexual sin. When word leaked out that I might have been drinking, rather than responding with humility and repentance, I was defiant. After all, I was twenty-seven years old. Who did people think they were policing my moral life? Those things were between me and God. What I didn't realize was that my struggle was beginning to take its toll on me. I was becoming more and more defensive and self-centered in my attitude. The war between flesh and spirit was wearing me down. And I was dangerously close to giving up.*

For many young Christians like Rich, the issue of moral failure centers on immaturity. They see adulthood and independence as a right to do whatever they please. When spiritual authority figures begin to confront them about their behavior, they often take great offense. Terms like "legalism" and "witch hunt" find their way into conversations. Ultimately, they grow tired of everyone being "in their business," and they stop fighting the sin.

Tragically, others simply see surrender as their only option.

Far too many Christians give up because they just get tired of fighting. In the midst of the internal struggle between flesh and spirit, they make a misguided calculation: Giving up must surely be easier than this. In order to find relief from the oppressive feelings of guilt and failure brought on by their sin, they simply stop fighting. And they soon discover a startling truth:

If you choose to give up, God will let you.

Letting go

Wes: I tried to gain victory over the drinking and sexual sin in my life for more than six months. It seemed like every time I made progress, I would fall again. My conversations with Rich always left me broken and repentant, but I could never seem to keep walking in victory. I tried going back to church and to college ministry events, but that didn't work either. When I would hear the music and the truth of the Word, it would tear me up inside. Finally, I decided I couldn't put myself through the emotional agony anymore. So I just gave in to the sin. It had to be easier than the hell I was living. I wish I had known then what I know now.

Lot must have been thinking the exact same thing as he gazed at the pillar of salt that had been his wife just the night before. She had disobeyed the angels' orders not to look back as the Lord unleashed His judgment on the city of Sodom. Now it was Lot who was looking back. How could it have come to this?

A few short years ago, he had left his ancestral home in Mesopotamia along with his uncle Abraham, his spiritual mentor. Abraham was the godliest man Lot had ever known, and he was sure to reap great benefits as his uncle's protégé. But somewhere along the way, Lot had taken a wrong turn. He soon knew it was wrong, but by that time, his life was like a runaway train, and he felt powerless to stop it. And so did Abraham.

Rich: Watching Wes sink into the lifestyle that he lived after high school was one of the hardest things I ever went through as a college pastor. It wasn't that I didn't understand what he was going through. It was that I understood all too well. I knew exactly where the road he was choosing would take him because I had once followed it. But making him understand that was next to impossible. All he could see was the pleasure his flesh was seeking and that it was right there for the taking. Fighting the good fight seemed to him like a lost cause. So he gave up. He had no idea what it would ultimately cost him.

This is often what happens when a Christian slips into sin. He never plans to make a train wreck of his life. But somewhere along the journey, he takes a wrong turn. Gradually, subtly, that wrong turn takes him farther and farther off the right course. Eventually, he becomes unable to see his way back to the main route, so he stops trying to get there. His life begins to pick up more speed along the wrong track, until one day he no longer cares where he is going. And that is a very dangerous way to live.

Calloused conscience

Rich: By 1992, I was far enough away from the path of God's will for my life that I could no longer see the point of trying. I was tired of living the endless cycle of guilt and confession. Alcohol was becoming a more regular part of my life. My church attendance was sporadic, and my spiritual strength was fading fast. So was my guilt. I no longer felt the intense remorse I had experienced that first night I failed morally. The tears of brokenness had all but dried up. My conscience had adjusted itself to a new lifestyle, one of pleasure-seeking and self-indulgence. For the most part, I didn't mind. Oh, there was the occasional thought that I needed to get back on track with the Lord, but I was convinced I would do that "someday." For now, I was having fun and doing whatever my heart desired. At least that's what I thought. What I didn't realize was that I was becoming a slave to my own flesh. And as I would soon find out, the flesh is the cruelest of taskmasters.

Sin does lead to guilt for a Christian. At first. But once sin becomes habitual, even a believer is not immune to the inevitable consequence: a calloused conscience. This is a term that refers to a person who no longer feels the same remorse over particular thoughts or actions that he used to feel. He may still possess a biblical "head knowledge" of right and wrong, but his moral standard of living has degenerated well below this level. And his conscience has lost the ability to feel guilty about it.

The law of diminishing returns takes its toll on the human conscience. When it is affected by the same stimulus over and over again, the conscience becomes less and less sensitive to that stimulus. Something that once triggered a strong guilt mechanism now produces little reaction at all. It is the same principle that causes the hands to develop calluses from swinging a golf club or working with tools. When something hits it in the same place enough times, the conscience can become calloused as well.

Wes: Once the pattern of drinking and immorality became established in my life, I got to the point where I no longer felt guilty about what I was doing. It wasn't that I didn't think it was wrong. Deep down, I knew I had no business living that way. But the truth is, I was enjoying my new lifestyle. If my flesh desired something, I didn't deny it. I guess you could say I was sowing all the wild oats I had not sown in high school. At first, it had been an emotional roller coaster. But now I was finally able to put any feelings of guilt out of my mind. I just distanced myself from any conversations or experiences that might trigger those kinds of feelings. Even my relationships with Rich, Chad, and Dane became distant and somewhat awkward. We still hung out from time to time, but the subject of my lifestyle and spiritual condition rarely came up. Once Chad actually confronted me about the way I was living. He told me he missed having me as a spiritual brother. The guy I had walked side by side with following Christ barely a year earlier was trying to bring me back to the Lord. I didn't say much to him, but I recall thinking I was living exactly like I wanted to. Looking back, it was an incredibly selfish way to live.

Sin does not ultimately lead to guilt. It only leads to more sin. The slippery slope both Rich and Wes found themselves on is one that many believers have slid down, only to find they were powerless to climb back up. In the opening chapter of his epistle to the Romans, the apostle Paul outlines the amazing phenomenon of how sin multiplies in a person's life. The closing verses of the chapter may be the most thorough description of this process ever penned:

> "Furthermore, just as they did not think it worthwhile to retain the knowledge of God, so God gave them over to a depraved mind, so that they do what ought not to be done. They have become filled with every kind of wickedness, evil, greed, and depravity. They are full of envy, murder, strife, deceit, and malice. They are gossips, slanderers, God-haters, insolent, arrogant, and boastful; they invent ways of doing evil; they disobey their parents; they have no understanding, no fidelity, no love, no mercy. Although they know God's righteous decree that those who do such things deserve death, they not only continue to do these very

things but also approve of those who practice them"
(Romans 1:28–32).

When a person's conscience becomes so seared that he no
longer has God in his conscious thoughts, his mind is wide open to
depravity. Only the presence of the Holy Spirit protects a Christian
from this same dynamic. And when the believer's habitual lifestyle
becomes one that constantly grieves the Holy Spirit, that believer is
just as open to a depraved mindset as an unsaved person. If he truly
belongs to Christ, he himself will never be lost, but his mind can
become so corrupted that he behaves as though he were. Later, in the
same letter to the Romans, Paul reminds believers of the importance
of maintaining spiritually healthy minds:

"And do not be conformed to this world, but be transformed by
the renewing of your mind" (Romans 12:2).

The battle of the Christian life is won or lost in the mind.
The King James translation of Proverbs 23:7 says, "For as (a man)
thinketh in his heart, so is he." The mind is an immensely powerful
vehicle in the life of a Christian. It can take him virtually anywhere.
Even to the greatest heights of his life.

And sometimes to the lowest depths.

Questions to consider:

Have you felt yourself being tempted to throw in the towel in the battle between your flesh and spirit?

Are there sin patterns in your life that you no longer feel guilty about?

Truth to embrace:

You must be willing to fight for the faith you possess.

"Fight the good fight of the faith. Take hold of the eternal life to which you were called when you made your good confession in the presence of many witnesses" (1 Timothy 6:12).

There is great reward at the end of every spiritual battle.

"Let us not become weary in doing good, for at the proper time we will reap a harvest if we do not give up" (Galatians 6:9).

A clear conscience is like the voice of God's Spirit.

"Cling to your faith in Christ, and keep your conscience clear. For some people have deliberately violated their consciences..." (1 Timothy 1:19 NLT).

Section Two: The Pit

> "I am counted with those who go down to the pit; I am like a man who has no strength"
> (Psalm 88:4 NKJV).

Chapter 4

Slipping into Darkness

As the mind goes, so goes the man. And the mind always goes somewhere. There is an old saying, "An idle mind is the Devil's workshop." That is only partially true. The mind can definitely become the Devil's workshop. But the mind is never idle.

Like any living entity, the mind craves nourishment. And food for the mind involves knowledge. When a person, Christian or otherwise, stops filling his mind with the knowledge of God, the mind will seek nourishment elsewhere. In the absence of God's truth, the mind will inevitably feed itself on the only alternative: the Enemy's lies.

This diet of deception leads to what the Bible refers to in the older translations as a "reprobate mind." That term essentially means a mind that thinks upside down. What it once believed to be right and true, it now believes to be wrong. And vice versa. This is what happens when a Christian begins to career down the slippery slope of sin. And where he ends up is a very dark place.

Blinded by the dark

> *Rich: I had always had a good head on my shoulders, morally speaking. I was the kid whose parents never had to give a curfew. I didn't 'drink, smoke, cuss, chew, or hang around with those who do.' That was true until my late twenties. Then it was like my mind and my morality just descended into a fog so thick and dark I didn't know my right from my left anymore. My perspective had become so distorted that crucial boundaries became blurred. Issues that used to be moral absolutes to me were now ambiguous at best. Behaviors like drinking and gambling now seemed like matters of personal preference rather than part of a moral standard. Oh, did I mention gambling? That habit had also crept into my life. It was a symptom of a much larger problem of financial irresponsibility that was slowly leading me down a path to disaster. My life was starting to unravel. I was nothing like the person who had been ordained a deacon in the church just three years before. And the scary part was, I could hardly even tell the difference.*

"Esau had to be out of his mind!" The thought kept running through Jacob's head as he watched his older brother gobble down the bowl of red stew. He knew Esau was impulsive; a "riverboat gambler" in our vernacular. But Jacob never dreamed that Esau was really foolish enough to take the deal he had half-jokingly offered a few moments earlier.

Esau had returned from one of his many all-day hunting trips exhausted and famished as usual. The smell of the stew Jacob had been cooking must have reached Esau's nostrils the moment he caught sight of the smoke rising from the fire in the waning sunlight. He burst into the tent and demanded that Jacob serve him a bowlful.

Being the shrewd negotiator that he was, Jacob couldn't pass up the opportunity to make his big brother squirm. "Sell me your birthright first."

It was an outlandish offer. No one in his right mind would dare give up the privilege of inheriting a double portion of their father Isaac's vast estate, not to mention the spiritual heritage and family authority that came along with it. Not for a bowl of stew. Esau was certainly no businessman, but he could at least discern the difference between a lifetime of blessing and a bowl of stew. No one would have taken Jacob's offer. No one in his right mind.

But Esau did. In an inexplicable lapse of judgment and sanity, the firstborn son of Isaac and Rebekah, the grandson and heir to the blessings of Abraham, traded his entire future for one measly bowl of red stew. It was an unbelievable transaction. No one would accept a fleeting, temporary thing like a bowl of stew in exchange for such a glorious future. Unless it was a future he could no longer see.

Wes: Once I turned my life over to sin, I really didn't think much about my future. When you're just living for the weekend or the next party, your future doesn't really enter your mind. You might as well be blind to it. You're just looking for the next moment of pleasure; the next hit of adrenaline. It's sad, but that's where a lot of people my age live their lives. Young adult culture is a vicious cycle of self-indulgence, and even a Christian can get sucked into it. I was proof of that. It looks inviting at first, but it gets old really quick. You start feeling emptier and emptier. And you look for anything to fill that void.

Misguided passion

Everyone longs for significance. Especially Christians. The Bible says of believers that we are God's workmanship. That means

He recreated us in Christ to be something of special significance as stewards of His kingdom in this world. Obviously, as Christ-followers, we know this true significance is found only in Him. That is the only place we should ever search for it. But it is when our walk descends into darkness that the search can lead us in some misguided directions.

Each of us is born with a void in his life that only Christ can fill. This "hole in our soul" is the emptiness many in the secular world attempt to fill up with all sorts of things, such as alcohol, drugs, relationships, money, and power. Although the Bible is clear that believers are complete in Christ, when a Christian makes a detour toward the darkness, he starts to feel the void again. Such fallen believers often attempt to fill this perceived emptiness with the same things the world turns to. And they aren't always sinful things in and of themselves.

Rich: In my pursuit of the sinful lifestyle I was now living, there came something I hadn't bargained for. When I left behind my church and my ministry, I had unintentionally left behind my greatest passion. A huge void was created in my life as a result. It was a hole that no amount of drinking, pornography, gambling or other self-indulgent pursuit could ever begin to fill. I needed something of genuine significance in my life. I thought I had found it in 1992 when some buddies and I decided to start a youth baseball organization. It was the perfect outlet. In fact, I had even figured out how it could help serve as a sort of penance for my spiritual shortcomings. We would put a Christian spin on it and place a premium on our leaders and coaches being positive role models for the kids. Don't get me wrong, I never set out to deceive anyone. I thought my motives were absolutely pure in the baseball endeavor, and I do believe God used it as a positive in a number of lives. Besides, I was determined to keep my private life a private matter. I could still be a role model by keeping up a good public image. And we enjoyed tremendous success, fielding seven teams that were highly competitive across the Southeast by our fourth year of existence. But despite our achievements and my "noble" intentions, baseball was not the passion God made me for. I was running full speed away from that.

Rich's experience illustrates one of the great tragedies of misguided passion. It isn't always the things we attempt to fill our voids with that are bad. The great tragedy is that we aren't running after the true passion we were made to pursue. We were all created for a divine purpose. For Christians, that purpose involves a specific kingdom assignment for our lives. Next to our salvation, discovering and fulfilling that God-given purpose is the most important thing about us.

Like so many devices of the Enemy, misguided passions divert our attention from our true purpose. Even when they aren't bad things, they serve to keep us from God's best. To be sure, one of the Enemy's favorite strategies for keeping us away from God is this type of distraction.

But make no mistake: His ultimate goal is our destruction.

Wes: Walking in darkness for me was about much more than being distracted. It was about self-destruction. When I walked away from the Lord, there was a hole left in my life that nothing could fill. I didn't fully realize it at the time, but everything I was doing was about trying to fill that void. The drinking, the sex, the partying—it was all an attempt to find something to live for. That's really what a lot of young adult culture is about. The chase for the next high, the next weekend, the next person to hook up with becomes the meaning of your life. And it just leads you deeper into darkness.

The search for life is common to man. The person who drinks is looking for life in a bottle. The drug addict is looking for life in a chemical high. The single person living a sexually active lifestyle is looking for life in the experience of pleasure and manufactured intimacy. The true Christian knows that genuine life is found only in relationship with the Son of God. But when a believer is out of fellowship with Christ, he becomes cut off from the practical expression of that life. And as he stumbles in the darkness, he ends up trying to replace it with the very same experiences as unsaved people.

Living the lie

A Christian living a hedonistic, pleasure-centered lifestyle is an oxymoron. The term "Christian" in its original form meant "little Christ." The thought of a miniature version of Jesus indulging in a sinful, self-serving lifestyle is blasphemous. How could someone whose very identity is inextricably tied to the Son of God dare to live a blatantly ungodly life? It is an equation that simply does not balance. Yet some Christians attempt to balance it.

By living two lives.

Rich: After we started the baseball organization, my options about how I lived my life were narrowed. Although I was no longer a regular church attendee, I was still under the scrutiny of the people who looked to me for leadership. By this time, I was too messed up spiritually to live a genuinely moral life. So I began living a double life. When I was with my baseball folks or making a rare appearance at church, I put on a good moral and spiritual facade. But when I was alone or with people I could let loose with, I was a completely different person. I can recall leaving baseball games or even church services and immediately heading to purchase pornography. I remember Sunday mornings when I showed up at church after being out all night indulging in all manner of immorality. It seemed for a while like I was getting away with it. But it was creating a horrible cycle of deception and fear in my life. I was living a

*lie. And I was terrified of being found out. The darkness was
closing in around me.*

When a Christian's life descends into darkness, he loses sight of
two very important things. The first is his moral direction. Not only
is his life characterized by poor moral choices, but his very ability
to discern morality is compromised. Even something as blatantly
dishonest as living a double life does not seem wrong to him. In
the book of Proverbs, Solomon described the moral condition of a
person whose life has descended into such a spiritual pit:

"But the way of the wicked is like deep darkness; they do not
know what makes them stumble" (Proverbs 4:19).

It is one thing for a Christian to knowingly disobey the will
of God. It is quite another when he loses the ability to recognize
his own disobedience. When this phenomenon occurs, his life can
do little but descend deeper into darkness and farther from any
sensible moral direction, until he has lost sight of something even
more precious:

His spiritual identity.

*Wes: The further I went into the spiritual darkness I was living
in, the less I even thought about what I might have been doing
wrong. It was a weird process, you know? Like I was descending
into deeper levels of sinfulness. At first, I knew what I was doing
was wrong, and I was really torn up about it. Then I reached
a point where I no longer felt guilty, but I still knew I wasn't
living right. I can remember going to buy beer at the store and
hoping no one I knew would see me because in my head I still
knew it was wrong. But somewhere along the way, you just
cross a point where nothing you're doing seems wrong anymore.
I think that's when you've lost sight of who you are. And that's
a terrible thing to lose.*

Esau went numb when he heard his father's words. He had just
returned from the hunt and had brought back game just as Isaac had

asked him to do. Now it was time to receive his inheritance. Isaac's words echoed over and over in Esau's head.

"I have made (Jacob) lord over you and have made all his relatives his servants, and I have sustained him with grain and new wine. So what can I possibly do for you, my son?" (Genesis 27:37).

Esau was sick, nauseated almost to the point of blacking out. Suddenly, his mind raced back to another day when he had returned from hunting and burst into that same tent. And as much as he wanted to plead with his father to grant him what had once been rightfully his, he knew it was a lost cause. He had thrown it all away a long time ago.

The man who had once been the firstborn son and heir of the richest man in Canaan now wept bitterly as he lay on his face by the bedside of his aging father. Just a few short years ago, he had such a bright future. Now he didn't even know who he was anymore. He had traded it all for one bowl of stew. And he had learned an excruciatingly painful lesson:

Your appetites can destroy you.

Questions to consider:

Are you allowing other passions to take the place of the one great purpose God made for you to pursue?

Do you find yourself acting and speaking differently at church and around Christians than you do in other settings?

Truth to embrace:

You will never find fulfillment apart from your God-given purpose.

"Yes, everything else is worthless when compared with the infinite value of knowing Christ Jesus my Lord. For his sake I have discarded everything else, counting it all as garbage, so that I could gain Christ" (Philippians 3:8 NLT).

A genuine Christian life is a biblically consistent life.

"Examine yourselves to see if your faith is genuine. Test yourselves. Surely you know that Jesus Christ is among you; if not, you have failed the test of genuine faith" (2 Corinthians 13:5 NLT).

Even things that are not sinful can often slow us down spiritually.

"Therefore, since we are surrounded by such a huge crowd of witnesses to the life of faith, let us strip off every weight that slows us down, especially the sin that so easily trips us up. And let us run with endurance the race God has set before us" (Hebrews 12:1 NLT).

Chapter 5

Eating with Pigs

> "The young man became so hungry that even the pods he
> was feeding the pigs looked good to him"
> (Luke 15:16 NLT).

It is amazing what a person will eat when he is starving. The more ravenous the appetite gets, the more bizarre its cravings become. If you get hungry enough, you will eat anything. Even pig slop.

A similar principle applies to spiritual hunger. When the spirit is being nourished by its proper food—the Word of God—it grows stronger and so does its desire for healthy nourishment. But when the spirit is deprived of its proper food, it grows weaker, and the appetite of the flesh is awakened. Like the spirit, when the flesh is fed what it wants, it grows stronger. In fact, it grows into a monster.

A monster whose appetites know no boundaries.

Bottomless pit

There is something about the appetite of the flesh that is different from that of the spirit. When the spirit is properly nourished, its appetite for the Word of God will grow, but the growth is healthy and reasonably paced. When the appetite of the flesh becomes enflamed, its growth is anything but healthy. It is malignant. And feeding it can be like trying to fill a void that only keeps getting larger.

Rich: Even with the success we had in baseball, my soul was never satisfied. The dream I had of building an organization that would genuinely help young people was never going to be realized with a leader who could not even help himself. I'm not saying there weren't some good times and some cherished memories that came out of the experience, but the deeper I went into it, the emptier I felt. It was no longer enough just to influence kids. Winning became my intoxicant, to the point that I found myself compromising principles in order to do it. But winning only satisfied me temporarily. Even in the midst of spiritual darkness, I could never hide from the reality that I was not doing what God made me to do. There was a huge void in my life, and it was growing.

Jesus often used word pictures to illustrate powerful truths about Himself. You might say He was the Master of it. He used these simple metaphors to explain deep spiritual truths to people who were not theologians. On one of these occasions, He called Himself the Bread of Life. It was an illustration to explain how He was the only "food" that could truly satisfy the hunger of the soul. Without that Bread, the soul's hunger can become overwhelming.

Wes: By the time I neared my twenty-first birthday, my life had descended into a cycle of drinking and sexual sin. My relationship with God was the furthest thing from my mind. I had not been to church in many months, and my relationships with my Christian brothers had become almost nonexistent. I worked with Rich on his second job occasionally, but we both knew spiritual conversations were pretty much pointless. I had enrolled in school and was working toward a career as an

X-ray technician. That and my partying lifestyle were all that mattered to me. I was desperately trying to fill the bottomless pit that was growing in my soul. Then one day, I got a call from the girl I had been seeing, and she dropped the bombshell. She was pregnant. I didn't even know how to respond. Marriage seemed out of the question. We had broken up months ago and had only seen each other a few times since then. It was like having the props kicked out from under me. I felt like my life was over.

The whirlpool of sin that seemed to engulf Wesley's life during that period was a manifestation of the emptiness that had been growing in his soul since he first walked away from the Lord. His spiritual hunger had not been satisfied in years, and he had forgotten what it was like to feed it. Now it was his flesh that screamed for constant nourishment, and its appetite was growing. And it was an appetite for destruction.

Insatiable hunger

The Holy Spirit through the pen of the apostle Paul said it best in the epistle to the Galatians:

"Whoever sows to please their flesh, from the flesh will reap destruction" (Galatians 6:8).

The young man had left home just a few months ago. Though not the firstborn son, he had stood to receive a healthy inheritance upon his father's death. But his father was in reasonably good health and likely had quite a few years left in him. And the boy was tired of waiting. A few months ago, he had boldly gone to his father and asked for his share of the family fortune right then and there.

It was an unheard of request in that culture. The disrespect alone would have been enough to make even the most brazen of rebels cringe. But amazingly, his father had granted his audacious request. As soon as his dad could get the money into his hands, the young man had packed his bags and set off on his own. Finally, he could live life his way, without his parents constantly preaching to him.

It had all sounded so good then. But not now. In just a few short months, the young man had foolishly spent his entire inheritance on drinking, gambling, and sensual pleasures. Now, not only was his money gone, he had absolutely nothing to show for it. To make matters worse, a famine had hit the country, and there was no work and very little food. Desperate for a place to stay, he had hired himself out to a pig farmer who let him sleep in the shed with the hogs.

He was broke, homeless, and desperately hungry. It seemed like only yesterday that he was feasting at his father's house. He longed for a home-cooked meal, but he was certain that would never happen again. He was so hungry he even found himself craving the food the pigs were eating.

The story of the Prodigal Son is one of the most beloved parables that Jesus ever told. We are all overwhelmed by the love and grace the father ultimately lavished on the younger son upon his return. But there are other elements in the story that we had best not overlook. Like what happens when we leave the security and blessing of unbroken fellowship with the father. And how, if we aren't careful, we can develop appetites for some unthinkable things.

Rich: Looking back, the thing that shocks me the most about my dark years is the appetite I developed for horribly ungodly things. As my emptiness continued to grow during the baseball years, I turned to pornography more and more. My failure to cultivate my relationship with God had left a huge void in my life. Pornography is often sought by men as a substitute for the authentic intimacy we all crave, and I was seeking it desperately. This was in the days before the widespread availability of Internet pornography, so I began spending hundreds of dollars and driving thousands of miles every month, seeking out new and different sexual highs from magazines and videos. I wouldn't dare purchase adult materials in my own part of town, so I often drove long distances for fear of being seen. This led to a number of all-night quests that caused me to miss work the next day. My attendance began to suffer as my lifestyle spun out of control. It sounds twisted, but going out at night on these hunts for X-rated materials became like an adventure. It was like I was literally becoming two different people. Besides, it was my only option. I could never have lived this lifestyle in the daylight.

Desperate deception

Rich was living the very life Job talked about when he said:

"The eye of the adulterer watches for dusk; he thinks, 'No eye will see me,' and he keeps his face concealed" (Job 24:15).

Men have an innate ability to compartmentalize their lives, and Rich was no exception. Living a double life may seem a bit psychotic at first glance, but most of us do this to one extent or another. It is not at all unusual for many Christians in our culture to live one way when we are at church with our brothers and sisters in Christ, while behaving very differently at work or on the golf course.

Rich also mentioned the chase for pornography becoming like an "adventure." The fact that he had to keep it hidden only served to heighten the adrenaline rush. This fed an aspect of his soul that is also uniquely male. God naturally wired men to crave adventure. We are reflections of the fierceness and boldness of our Creator. All of us long to achieve and to accomplish something meaningful with our lives. When we aren't pursuing the lives God made us for, our hunger for significance often ends up being fed through some ungodly means.

Or sometimes, we simply medicate it away.

Wes: In the months after I learned of the pregnancy, I descended into a dark abyss of apathy and self-pity. I was no longer just living for the weekend. I was living to get off work, so I could go out and drink. Any future I might have been dreaming of was gone as far as I was concerned, and my life became a search to anesthetize my feelings of despair and emptiness. I became so engulfed in this self-absorbed lifestyle of partying that I was literally going out five nights a week to get drunk. I didn't care about anything else. Soon my grades began to suffer, and a month before my son was born, I got kicked out of radiography school. I was living with my parents at the time, and I was too ashamed to tell them what had happened. So every morning, I would get up and pretend to go to school, but would really just go to different friends' houses. I would hang out wherever I could until late at night, and then come home and start the whole charade again. Some nights, if my dad was still awake, I would sleep in the car so he wouldn't see me in my messed-up condition. I was living a lie, and it was slowly but surely sucking the life out of me.

Wesley's desperation to cover his expulsion from college was not unlike the double life Rich lived during his struggle with pornography. In both cases, they were attempting to do something many believers do every single day that is ultimately a human impossibility:

They were attempting to cover their own sin.

Even King David was not immune to such desperate measures. As was the case with Wes, the news of an unexpected pregnancy had sent David into a tailspin. He couldn't have a child by this woman. She was another man's wife! What would the people think of their spiritual leader? What would the political fallout be if the Lord's anointed were discovered in such a sordid affair?

As the king pondered these questions, a strange but all too common phenomenon occurred. Rather than do what any believer knows he should do in such a situation—confess his sin—David began thinking of how he could cover it up. And that is exactly what he attempted to do. He would live to regret that decision.

Bathsheba's husband, Uriah the Hittite, was on the battlefield, leading a regiment of David's soldiers in combat against Israel's enemies. No doubt he missed his wife. This gave David an idea, a devious and ungodly idea. But in his state of spiritual desperation, David had no idea just how ungodly it would become. He would give Uriah a three-day furlough and let him come home. Uriah was certain to sleep with Bathsheba, and when the baby was born, no one would suspect David was the father. It seemed like a foolproof plan.

But as so often happens when one of God's children takes matters into his own hands, it quickly spiraled out of control. Uriah slept on his doorstep, refusing to go in to his wife's bed while his soldiers slept on the battlefield. The next night David brought Uriah to the palace and got him drunk, sure that alcohol would send him home to sleep with Bathsheba. But even drunk, Uriah proved to be of sounder mind and superior character than the conniving David was sober. He again slept on the porch.

It is then that David's scheme took a sinister and cold-blooded turn. The next morning, he handed Uriah an envelope with sealed orders to be given to the commanding general. Upon his return to the battle, Uriah gave the envelope to General Joab, who opened it and read the following words that still bring a chill to the stoutest of hearts:

"Put Uriah out in front where the fighting is fiercest. Then withdraw from him so he will be struck down and die." (2 Samuel 11:15).

David's desperation had reached the point of no return. The man after God's own heart was no longer merely an adulterer. He was a murderer. In his youth, he had struck down Goliath, Israel's mortal enemy, for blaspheming the name of the Lord. Now he had struck down Uriah, a good man, for honoring his king and his country. It was an unfathomable turn of events. King David had fallen further than anyone ever dreamed he could.

And he was powerless to get back up.

Questions to consider:

Have you found yourself developing appetites for things you never thought you would desire?

Are there behavioral patterns in your life that you have expended a great deal of energy trying to hide from certain people?

Truth to embrace:

Left unchecked, our appetites can destroy us.

"For, as I have often told you before and now tell you again even with tears, many live as enemies of the cross of Christ. Their destiny is destruction, their god is their stomach, and their glory is in their shame" (Philippians 3:18–19).

As believers, we do not have to submit to our appetites.

"Those who belong to Christ Jesus have crucified the flesh with its passions and desires" (Galatians 5:24).

"Hiding" from God is a fruitless effort that only leads to pain.

"Have nothing to do with the fruitless deeds of darkness, but rather expose them. It is shameful even to mention what the disobedient do in secret" (Ephesians 5:11–12).

Chapter 6

Sinking to Rise No More

"I sink in the miry depths, where there is no foothold. I have come into the deep waters; the floods engulf me" (Psalm 69:2).

A life of sin takes its toll. That is as true of a Christian as it is of a nonbeliever. Even one who is washed in the blood of the Lamb is not exempt from the earthly consequences of sinful choices. When those choices become a lifestyle, the consequences can be far-reaching.

Even debilitating.

Down to despair

Rich: By the spring of 1997, the life I had been living was beginning to have devastating effects on me. Not only was my spiritual life and ministry in shambles, but my finances were as well. Before I began to stray from the Lord, I had no debt and several thousand dollars in the bank. By the time I was thirty-three, I was staring at nearly $60,000 of mostly unsecured debt. It was the sorry residual of a grossly irresponsible, self-indulgent *life. The baseball organization I had labored to build was on the verge of financial insolvency. Any future I might have once dreamed of now seemed like a distant memory. I would never own a home or even be able to support myself. I was living in a basement apartment at my grandparents' house. I helped with the bills, but I still felt like a complete failure in life. I sought almost constant escape from the inner pain I was feeling. My pornography problem had grown to the point that it was no longer a struggle. It was an addiction.*

An addiction is a baffling thing. It is a strange, inexplicable bond that people develop with something that is out to destroy them. They love it and hate it at the same time. Although the addiction is leading them down the path to destruction, they continue to seek out and indulge in the behavior, even to their own detriment.

For Rich, this phenomenon first became obvious in his battle with pornography. But it was present in other areas of his life—in particular, his finances. Addictions can involve anything that possesses the potential to control you. The consequences almost always manifest themselves in a gradually diminishing quality of life. But sometimes they can even be immediate.

Wes: The year after my son was born was definitely a low point. He was a beautiful, healthy kid, and I was grateful for that, but I was still hopelessly focused on myself and the future I was certain I had thrown away. Late that summer, my parents told me I had to get a job or move out. I had finally told them about the school thing, but I had no steady source of income. I ended up moving in with some guys I partied with. I had lived with people who weren't following Christ before, but this was different. This time I had moved into the pit of hell. I started drinking literally every night. Usually I would drink at the house, but it was not uncommon for me to go out and drink and then drive home, regardless of how much I'd had. Then one night it happened. I got pulled over and charged with DUI. I had no idea at the time, but God was going to use that event in my life for great glory down the road. You would think it might have been a wake-up call, but it wasn't. I was way too far gone for that.

You would think the death of Uriah might have awakened King David from his spiritual slumber as well. But it didn't. Joab (one of David's "yes men") had carried out his orders to perfection. He had placed Uriah on the front lines, and when the fighting was at its fiercest, he had ordered his men to retreat from Uriah. It was a certain death sentence for an innocent man. And it was a direct order from King David himself.

When Joab sent word of the battle back to the king, he was confident of David's reaction. He instructed the messenger not to worry if the king became angry over the army's defeat, but to simply mention that Uriah the Hittite had perished in the battle. King David would certainly be pleased to hear that. This macabre prediction played out exactly as Joab expected.

> The messenger said to David, "The men overpowered us and came out against us in the open, but we drove them back to the entrance of the city gate. Then the archers shot arrows at your servants from the wall, and some of the king's men died. Moreover, your servant Uriah the Hittite is dead."
>
> David told the messenger, "Say this to Joab: 'Don't let this upset you; the sword devours one as well as another. Press the attack against the city and destroy it.' Say this to encourage Joab" (2 Samuel 11:23–25).

The cowardly murder of one of his bravest soldiers should have awakened David from his nightmare of sin, but it did not. In fact, there is no indication that he felt any remorse at all during the months that followed. He took Bathsheba to be his wife, and all returned to normal in the kingdom of Israel.

But standing quietly in the background; watching the entire saga unfold, was a man named Nathan. He was God's prophet and spiritual advisor to the king, much as Samuel had been to Saul. He was a godly man; a man of great spiritual discernment.

And he could discern what lay ahead for David.

Bound and gagged

The Enemy has one goal in your life. It is not to tempt you. It is not to present an alternative to God or to offer you pleasure with a price tag. It is to destroy you. A familiar but perhaps slightly misunderstood passage makes this abundantly clear:

"The thief comes only to steal and kill and destroy; I have come that they may have life, and have it to the full" (John 10:10).

Notice carefully the language: The thief does not merely come to steal and kill and destroy. He comes *only* to do these things. Satan's ultimate goal in the life of any person is destruction. For a nonbeliever, that goal involves the eternal destruction of his soul in hell. But do not be deceived. The Enemy desires destruction for Christians as well. In fact, he desires it especially for Christians.

A believer's eternal soul is safe from the Devil's destruction. John's gospel makes this clear in the very same passage:

"I give them eternal life, and they shall never perish" (John 10:28).

Speaking of the saved, John essentially said that no one—including Satan—could ever take away the eternal life they have in Christ. But many believers make the tragic and foolish assumption that their lives on this earth are somehow exempt from destruction as well. Nothing could be further from the truth. Satan loves nothing more than to stifle the expression of eternal life in a Christian until he can extinguish his physical life.

He loves to steal, kill, and destroy. Christians are his favorite targets. And he is relentless in his attacks.

Rich: Sin is never satisfied. If I learned anything during my dark journey, it is that sin is never content with any level of control over our lives. I had reached the point of realizing that I was addicted to pornography. I had heard people say it was a drug. They were absolutely right. Few behaviors are as addictive or as demoralizing as sexual sin. Yet even in the midst of this stronghold, I was still so empty that I wanted something else to satisfy me. That's when I turned to prescription drugs. It is easy to see now how people become addicted to painkillers. They are just so easy to get. But they can also become expensive. And when you're already spending huge amounts of money gambling, buying pornography, and feeding your emptiness, they can just about bankrupt you. But when you're desperate you don't care. You just want to feel good. This works for a while, and then the law of diminishing returns kicks in. After that, you're just trying not to feel at all.

"Not feeling at all" is a good way to describe a person who has almost reached the proverbial "rock bottom" of life. Rich was clearly at the point where he cared about little but himself. It is a terrible way to approach living and is literally poison to anything good in your life.

Or in your future.

Wes: I can remember after I got the DUI that it didn't even bother me that much. I mean, it did cause me some legal problems, but it really didn't affect me emotionally or spiritually. I figured, "Why should it bother me?" As far as I was concerned, my future was blown to pieces. There didn't seem to be anything to plan or prepare for, so I did what made the most sense to me. I just lived for the moment. For me, that meant living to drink. Of course, when I moved into that house, other things started to come into the picture. Drugs were literally all around me, and pretty soon, I started smoking some weed. Over the next year or so, I tried virtually every drug you could imagine. Before I knew it, I was not only drinking, but getting high every night. This new wrinkle in my lifestyle was not only taking me deeper into sin, but also costing me more money. I had gotten a decent job, but I was spending my whole paycheck on partying. Many times, I would drink all night, and then wake up just in time to get to work. I know there were days when I must have come in reeking of alcohol. As I think back on it, it's a small miracle my lifestyle didn't cost me my job. My finances were a wreck. I ended up getting some credit cards and running up those. It didn't take long before I was deep in debt, and the creditors were calling.

Faces of death

Sin's goal is most definitely the destruction of your life. It can accomplish that in any number of ways, such as attacking and destroying relationships, careers, finances, and families. But make no mistake: Its favorite vehicle is death. James 1:15 tells us, "Sin, when it is full-grown, gives birth to death." If sin can't rob you of eternal life, it will settle for taking your physical life.

Rich: When you're in your early thirties, you seldom think about dying. Even when your life spirals out of control in the darkness, you take for granted that you will live to see the light of day. The pursuit of pornography is strikingly similar to the "chase" for drugs I have heard addicts describe. It makes you take risks you would never take in your right mind. My addiction to pornography had taken me to some dark places; darker than I ever thought I would be in. But it was my addiction to drugs that would eventually take me to some dangerous places. Unlike pornography, my drug habit initially did not require me to conduct business under cover of darkness. Fortunately, my addiction was not clinical, it was only emotional. I was able to procure painkillers either by prescription or through acquaintances. But as the habit grew, acquaintances led to "connections." And "connections" (who are essentially street dealers) can lead to danger. I began engaging in some extremely stupid and risky behavior. It was nothing for me to be out at two or three o'clock in the morning. One night, I very foolishly allowed one of these "connections" into my vehicle. I had dealt with him a couple of times, and he had seemed friendly enough. But this night was different. He asked if I could give him a ride downtown. Along the way, he somehow became convinced that I had tried to cheat him. I knew I hadn't, but it was my word against his. The next thing I knew, he had pulled a large knife out of his pocket, looked at me, and said, "Let's see what you got." My heart sank to the pit of my stomach. I was unarmed, and I had no more cash to give him. This person I didn't even know was holding my life in his hands, and I had nowhere to run. I can't explain what happened next, but somehow I was able to convince him to get out of the car. I drove home in a cold sweat. All that night, I lay awake, terrified and ashamed beyond imagination. I had nearly thrown my very life away over a stupid habit. I cried out to the Lord that night, but I wasn't sure He was even listening.

Death is no respecter of persons. It is a strange phenomenon, but when a Christian who possesses eternal life walks away from Christ, he essentially moves into fellowship with death. David wrote about this dynamic in the Psalms:

"If I ascend to heaven, You are there;

If I make my bed in Sheol, behold, You are there" (Psalm 139:8 NASB).

To an Old Testament Jew, Sheol was the dwelling place of the dead. It was the equivalent of Hades in Greek mythology. In

Psalm 139:8, David was using the hypothetical comparison between a person who pursued fellowship with God ("ascend to heaven") and one who ran away from Him ("make my bed in Sheol"). The figurative path to Sheol bears the footprints of many. Even some who belonged to the Lord.

> *Wes: Life in the house I had moved into was about as different as you could imagine from the life I had once lived. It was one constant party. The level of filth I was living in, both spiritually and physically, was suffocating. It was a place that had become notorious to everyone from drug dealers to law enforcement. One night, there was a guy at the house who I knew was into drugs. I was drunk, and we had gotten into an argument over something. I don't even remember what about now, but he just kept yelling and getting more out of control. All of a sudden, he pulled a gun. Everybody in the room froze. I just reacted instinctively. I lunged at him and punched him in the face just as he had cocked the gun and was raising it toward me. I blacked out after that. Then the other guys jumped on him and got the gun. It was crazy. Like my life flashing before my eyes.*

The wages of sin is death. This is true on several levels. To Adam and Eve, as well as every human being born thereafter, it meant spiritual death. To a person who rejects Jesus Christ, it means eternal death. To a believer, it could mean physical death. But it could also mean the death of God's purpose and plan for his life. And that is a death that causes tremendous grief. A grief that many never get over.

When a Christian who has turned his back on God is suddenly faced with his own mortality, the impact can be sobering. A realization that has long been neglected hits home: the fact that he has been useless to the kingdom of God. For both Rich and Wes, that realization would eventually come. The God-ordained destinies they had each dreamed of fulfilling were no longer in the picture.

Resiliency is supposed to be a hallmark of a man of God. When he gets knocked down by life, he is supposed to seek the Lord, and then get up and get back in the game. King Solomon even wrote about this character quality:

"For though the righteous fall seven times, they rise again" (Proverbs 24:16).

We read these powerful words, and their truth stirs our hearts. But for far too many broken believers, there comes a point where getting up just no longer seems worth the effort. Rich and Wes both crossed that point in their journeys. There was simply no point in trying anymore. Besides, God was hardly even on their radar.

Little did they know, they had never left His.

Questions to consider:

When you think about your future, do you see it as bright and filled with promise or hopeless and limited?

Have you ever lost hope that God can and will still use you to your full potential in His kingdom?

Truth to embrace:

A believer's future is never hopeless.

"There is surely a future hope for you, and your hope will not be cut off" (Proverbs 23:18).

Grace can enable us to take back what the Enemy has stolen.

"So I will restore to you the years that the swarming locust has eaten" (Joel 2:25 NKJV).

When we walk with Christ, we have victory over death.

"The Lord protects those of childlike faith; I was facing death, and he saved me. Let my soul be at rest again, for the Lord has been good to me" (Psalm 116:6–7 NLT).

Section Three: The Rescue

"Reach down your hand from on high; deliver me and rescue
me from the mighty waters"
(Psalm 144:7).

Chapter 7

Hand of God

It is not terribly uncommon in our culture for someone to wreck his life. But it presents a whole different dynamic when that person is a Christian. The Bible never indicates that the life of a believer will be free from the presence of sin or that a Christian cannot struggle in his walk for a season. Much has been debated among the denominations throughout the centuries about whether or not a person who seems to temporarily abandon the practice of his faith was ever a believer to begin with. For Rich and Wes, there simply is no debate.

Preserved

Rich: Even though I fell so far away from whom I had once been, there was never a doubt in my mind that I belonged to Christ. I know it may seem unthinkable to some people that a believer could ever stray as far as I did, but all I can tell you is, as much death as I was living in, my spirit was still alive to God. There were many periods during those five years when I was woefully unaware of that reality, but I still maintain I was His. As He promised in His Word, "I will never leave you nor forsake you." I can tell you now I know that is true just as sure as I know the sun rises in the east. Looking back on my dark years, the way God preserved and protected me has been one of the greatest affirmations of my faith. There is no way I could have survived those years, spiritually or physically, if He had not been watching over me in the dark.

In Psalm 139, one of the greatest passages ever penned on the sustaining presence and faithfulness of God, David talked about how a believer can never completely escape the reality that he belongs to the Lord.

> "If I go up to the heavens, you are there; if I make my bed in the depths, you are there. If I rise on the wings of the dawn, if I settle on the far side of the sea, even there your hand will guide me, your right hand will hold me fast. If I say, 'Surely the darkness will hide me and the light become night around me,' even the darkness will not be dark to you; the night will shine like the day, for darkness is as light to you" (Psalm 139:8–12).

It is almost humorous to consider the notion of a Christian attempting to hide from God in the dark. Yet that is what many who stray from the path try to do. They become deceived into thinking that, by fooling people, they are somehow fooling God. But even in their vain efforts to escape God's presence, He is there. He never leaves them. He never stops thinking about them. And He never forgets they are His.

Wes: It's an absolute miracle that I lived to tell this story. Not only could I have been killed from driving drunk or being surrounded by violent people, I also could have killed myself. I was immersed in a culture of drugs and alcohol. I drank literally every night, and I smoked a lot of marijuana. But by a miracle of God, I never became addicted to drugs. There were guys I lived with who were badly addicted. And it wasn't that I didn't try stuff. I never used a needle or did acid, but I tried about every other drug there was. The way I was living, it would have made perfect sense if I had OD'd or had become an addict. But all I can say is, God was watching over me. He knew I was His, and He still had a plan for my life. It's almost too much to think about sometimes.

The grace of God is truly an unfathomable thing. The fact that He would extend mercy to anyone is beyond amazing. But the idea that God would show grace to a Christian who has train-wrecked his life is even further outside the realm of the sensible. In fact, it is more than some people can believe.

In his first epistle to Timothy, the apostle Paul talks about his life before he became a follower of Christ:

"Even though I was once a blasphemer and a persecutor and a violent man, I was shown mercy because I acted in ignorance and unbelief" (1 Timothy 1:13).

We all celebrate the grace God showed to Paul. What an amazing Savior who would extend mercy to a sinner so vile as one who would murder the servants of Christ! Believers embrace this grace as God's undeserved forgiveness and redemption toward those who have known only unbelief and ignorance of the true gospel.

But what about those who aren't ignorant? Does the mercy and forgiveness of a holy God toward vile sinners apply when the vile sinner in question is a Christian? For many people in our world today, this question is at the very crux of their reality. Will God really extend grace and restoration to believers who have somehow ended up in a spiritual pit? Many Christians today are paralyzed by this question and are desperately hoping for God to give the answer.

His answers always come in the nick of time.

Midnight madness

Most people who fall away have to reach a point where reality smacks them before they turn back to God. And that almost always means hitting bottom. For the Prodigal Son, that moment came when he lay in the squalor of a pigpen, starving to death. The Bible says he had an epiphany:

"When he came to his senses, he said, 'How many of my father's hired servants have food to spare, and here I am starving to death'"(Luke 15:17).

For a true child of God, the low point always comes. The moment of realization can sometimes be sudden. In other cases, it occurs in stages. More often than not, there is outside help involved.

Rich: The year my life began to turn around was 1997. Since I was a teenager, I had worked closely with my high school's football program as their media and statistics person. After I graduated, my role had expanded into a sort of unofficial chaplain for the team. I would pray with the guys before games and was a daily presence at practice just to be there and show support.

By the time the 1997 season began, my spiritual impact on the football team had become minimal. Those kinds of things just had not been a high priority to me, and I was not living nearly the kind of spiritual life that would lend itself to being very helpful to others. But as the season progressed, something began to stir in my spirit. To this day, I don't know how to explain it other than to say the Spirit of God was bearing witness with my spirit that it was time to wake up. My self-absorbed heart was starting to feel a burden for the guys on that '97 football team. But who was I to offer any spiritual guidance? I was a mess.

Then one night, God decided it was time to start cleaning up the mess. I was lying in bed just before midnight when I heard a knock at my door. Understanding what my life had been like the past five years, a midnight knock was not exactly a welcome noise. I went to the door and there stood CH Qualls, a former football player who was now doing ministry to middle school kids. Why in the world was this college guy rousing me out of bed? It so happened that during the same 1997 football season that God was tugging at my dead heart for the souls of those players, He had been speaking to CH about starting some kind of Bible study with the high school guys. CH told me I was the first person that popped into his head to help lead it. He shared with me how I had influenced him and his teammates when they were in school. Was he serious? Did he really have no idea that I was in no shape to lead something like that? I was confused, but somehow energized at the same time. I didn't know quite what to make of CH and this midnight visitation. Little did I know then, but he might as well have been an angel dispatched directly from the throne of God.

What Rich was experiencing that October night was the amazing, rescuing grace of a Father who never forgets his children. And God's mercy is as great toward a fallen Christian as it is toward the most repentant of sinners, responding to the gospel. The fountain of grace that springs forth at the cross of Jesus Christ flows in all directions. From the foot of the cross, it flows to wash clean the past of those who have come to receive the gospel. And its flow is just as powerful beyond the cross to cleanse, restore, and revive those who have already been there.

No matter where their journey has taken them.

Rich's long process of spiritual healing would begin during that autumn in 1997. It would be a gloriously difficult journey that would ultimately take him to the greatest heights of his spiritual life. And more than a decade later, he would have an opportunity to be a door-holder to help change another life forever.

Wes: The summer I turned twenty-three was undoubtedly my lowest point. There was just no purpose to my life anymore. It was hard to even call what I was to my son a father. Not that I didn't love my son, but I was really just a guy paying child support and working to stay alive. And I mostly stayed alive to drink. Oh yeah, the DUI. In September 2009 (remember that date), I had to go to the courthouse to pay a fine associated with the DUI. I went to the clerk's office and paid my fee. Just before I left the building, I heard someone yell at me from the upstairs balcony. It was Chad. I couldn't believe my eyes. I hadn't seen him, Dane, or Rich in forever. Chad had just gotten married a few weeks earlier, and I didn't even go to the wedding. He motioned for me to come upstairs. Turns out, he had gotten a job working at the courthouse. We talked for a few minutes, and then he told me that Rich worked there in the same department and that I should stop by and see him. I walked into Rich's office, feeling really uncomfortable. I didn't feel like those guys were a part of my life or even cared about me anymore. After a few minutes of pretty awkward conversation, I said I needed to get going. Chad walked me to the elevator, and just before I got on, he stuck something in my hand. "This is for you, man." I didn't know what to say. It was a sealed envelope with my name typed on the outside. I took it back to my car, sat down in the driver's seat, and opened it. I barely started reading the letter before the tears began to flow.

August 17, 2009
Dear Wes,

I'm honestly not sure exactly what I'm doing right now. I only know that there's a lot overflowing from my heart, and since I haven't had the chance to say any of it in person, I'm just going to have to put it on paper.

Needless to say, this has been one of the most emotional weeks of my life. Chad's wedding has been for me a whirlwind of pride, joy, thanksgiving, and sadness. It was the proudest and most joyous moment of my life to stand there at the altar and charge him with taking care of the woman God brought into his life. And there was a sadness almost beyond words at the realization that there was something missing. Wes, I know I don't tell you anything you don't already know when I say that not having you there as a part of Chad's wedding was like a missing piece of a beautiful picture. Never in my wildest dreams would I have thought of one of you getting married without the other as part of the process. But sometimes life itself can be stranger than dreams.

I'm just going to say some things to you that I've never really had the chance to say face to face—at least not in a very long time. I make no promises that this will all come out perfectly. It is a mixture of strong spiritual conviction and powerful heartfelt emotion. But here goes. Very vivid in my mind is the image of a young man who loved God deeply and passionately. Who wanted very much to live a life that would honor Him. Who wanted someday to have a godly wife and kids that he would take to church, model Christ for, and lead spiritually as a true man of God. That image is still very much alive in my mind today. And it is an image that bears your face.

As I said, that image is very much alive in my mind. It is not, however, what I see when I look at you. Please understand that brutally honest is what I have to be right now. Wes, when I look at you, I see a young man who is very deceived. A few years ago, he was everything I described in the preceding paragraph. And his Enemy set a bullseye on him and took him down. It shouldn't have been a shock. It happens every day.

And now when I look at you I see a young man very deceived. Deceived into believing some powerful lies about himself. Deceived into believing he could never be who he once could have been. Deceived into believing that it doesn't matter anymore. Deceived into believing that "life" lies somewhere outside the parameters of true godliness. Deceived into believing that "ordinary" is as good as he's ever going to be.

I don't know how precisely accurate any of that is. But I can tell you it's exactly how things look from this side of the fence. Wesley, I can only begin to imagine how much water has gone under your bridge since the days when we walked side by side with God. I know you've been through and experienced far more things now than the boy I once counseled and mentored. But I also know something else. I know I've been every bit as far off the path as you.

I just feel like I need to say this to you. I have been in as deep a pit as any Christian ever fell into. More water than you can ever fathom has gone under my bridge. But I also need you to know this. There are many ways into a pit—but there is only one way out. It doesn't involve more digging. It isn't about finding a different part of the pit to live in, or just flat-out getting used to life in the pit. It's about giving up and taking the hand of the only One who can pull us out. I did that twelve years ago. I know exactly where I was then. I don't know exactly where you are now. But I can assure you that God does. And I can also say to you with great conviction that there has never been a moment when I did not hold fast to the belief that you belong to Him. I believe that even now as I sit here at midnight typing this letter.

Wes, like I said, I don't presume to know where you are in relation to where you used to be or need to be. But I know I can no longer ignore the Spirit inside me that won't let me rest until I say these things. Because I believe tonight that God's light is going to shine through the deception. I believe that Wesley Shropshire is going to get a glimpse of the man God has always dreamed he would be. I believe your son is going to grow up to know a father who loves God and teaches him to love Him. I believe a man is going to emerge who will overcome the pit and live for the glory the Enemy thinks he stole. Do not be deceived. He has stolen nothing God cannot completely restore.

I can't write much more. But I do want to say just a few more things. Wesley, there has been a piece of my heart missing without you in my life these past couple of years. I have been in ministry for twenty-three years, and I have walked with literally hundreds of kids. No one has ever been more like a son to me than Wesley Shropshire. I love you with all of my heart, and you will always have a special place in it. I don't yet know what will become of this letter. I only pray that God will bless it to find its way into your hands, and that He will open your heart as you read it. The rest of the deal is yours. I will be here for you for whatever and whenever you need me. Remember who you are, Wes. God has not forgotten. And neither have I.

I love you,
Rich

I sat in my car sobbing like a baby for what seemed like an hour. It was like God was speaking to me for real for the first time in so long. I wanted to respond to Him right then, but there was just so much junk. I didn't know it that day, but my life was about to be completely turned upside down by His grace.

No postage necessary

Rich's letter to Wes was intensely personal yet filled with biblical truth. It represents the bold and unashamed manner in which God wants us to love one another as brothers and sisters in Christ. As our pastor, Dr. Rocky Ramsey, has said, "Every believer needs someone who will come alongside them and say 'You can do this; I believe in you, and you are not alone.' "

The letter and the story behind it is not only a testimony to the amazing grace and unconditional love of our heavenly Father toward His children. It is much more than that. It is the story of a miracle.

Rich: I was driving home one Monday night from Vision, our college ministry meeting, when God unmistakably spoke to my heart that I needed to write Wes a letter. So I got home, sat down at my computer, and for the next thirty minutes poured out a story of hope, love, forgiveness, and restoration that came straight from the heart of God through my fingers. There was only one problem. I had no idea how to get it to Wes. I had not seen him in almost a year. He was no longer living at home, and I had no way to contact him since he had long since lost his cell phone. So I just prayed that God would make a way. Then I did something that to this day I cannot explain. I took the letter to work with me. I work at the county courthouse, so I have no idea how I thought that would help, but I laid it on my desk behind my monitor and that is where it stayed for almost a month. I remember the day like it was yesterday. I came in to work and noticed that letter, collecting dust behind my computer screen. I just stopped and prayed right there in the middle of my office. I confessed that I had no way to get that letter into Wesley's hands myself, and I just told God that if it was supposed to get there, He would have to do it. Less than three hours later, I looked up from my desk, and there out my window, in another part of our office, stood Wes.

Neither Rich nor Wes was looking for grace. They were merely existing from one day to the next, assuming life would never be any different. But grace was looking for them. And when the God of all grace puts one of His children in His crosshairs, escape is not an option. Grace will find you.

Wherever you are.

Questions to consider:

Do you need to confess and repent of a time of spiritual darkness in your life?

Is there some brother, sister, pastor, or mentor in Christ that you need to reconnect with?

Truth to embrace:

If we repent, God will always offer us reconciliation.

"Therefore tell the people: 'This is what the Lord Almighty says: "Return to me," declares the Lord Almighty, "and I will return to you," says the Lord Almighty' "(Zechariah 1:3).

If we will return to Him in humility, God will wash away all our sin.

"'Come now, and let us reason together,' says the Lord.
'Though your sins are like scarlet,
They shall be as white as snow;
Though they are red like crimson,
They shall be as wool'" (Isaiah 1:18 NKJV).

Chapter 8

One Small Step

> "I will arise and go to
> my father"
> (Luke 15:18 NKJV).

American astronaut Neil Armstrong, the first man to walk on the moon, immortalized the words, "One small step for man; one giant leap for mankind." The exaggerated comparison of a small step and a giant leap captured perfectly the significance of human beings setting foot on the moon for the first time in history. The same comparison could be applied to a wayward believer returning to God. It only takes a small step.

A small step that feels like a giant leap.

I will arise

The Prodigal Son had finally come to his senses. He knew it was time to go home. But home was a place where he could hardly imagine himself ever being again. How could he possibly go back to his father after what he had done? After the person he had become?

74

Maybe if he stated his case humbly enough, his father might accept him back as a field hand. Surely he could never be a son again. It was going to be the hardest step of his life. But he had to take it.

Rich: After CH left my house that night, I did some pretty serious praying. You might say I was on my face before God. I didn't even know how to put into words the magnitude of all I had done against Him. But despite it all, I could hear His voice again. I knew He was calling me to do something with this Bible study idea that CH had thrown out. I had no idea what the future held as I knelt that night, but I knew I had to somehow walk away from the past I had created. I asked the Lord to forgive me that night. On the authority of His Word, I knew He would. But believing it in a practical sense would be much more challenging. The issue of leading a Bible study was another matter entirely. I was far less convinced that God could or would ever use me for anything significant again. I realize now I was doing exactly what the Prodigal did. I assumed that God would take me back as a hired servant, but never as a son.

Taking that first step toward God is the very essence of repentance. It takes more than merely confessing your sins and asking for God's forgiveness to change your life. There must be a change of thinking that leads to a change of behavior. In fact the Greek word for repentance, metanoeo, literally means "to think again." We must rethink the way we are living, to the point that we actually begin to change it. This goes significantly beyond merely confessing our sin. Confession is only the first part of a two-step process that many struggling Christians never complete. They never get to step two:

The small step back toward God.

Wes: During the weeks after I got the letter from Rich, I thought about my relationship with God numerous times. But it would always fade away with my nightly routine of partying. Then, Thanksgiving weekend, something in my heart gave way. I just couldn't bring myself to do the drinking or anything else that weekend. I locked myself in my room, away from all the junk, and just poured out my heart to God. I knew it was time to grow up and start becoming the man I was made to be. But it was going to have to start with getting out of that house. Moving in with my girlfriend was an option, but I knew that was out of the question. Besides, I needed a place where I could be held accountable and really have a chance to heal spiritually. The first person I thought about calling was Rich. He had recently built a house and had a couple of spare rooms. Chad had lived there up until he got married, and I knew it was the place for me. But after everything that had gone down in the past few years, I was really nervous about calling Rich, let alone asking him if I could live there. It was a step I was just going to have to man up and take.

"Man up" is a term that it doesn't take a seminary degree to relate to. Sometimes there is an element to true repentance that isn't particularly mystical or theological. It just involves "manning up" and doing what you know you need to do. And for a Christian returning to the Lord, it isn't about doing anything in our own strength. It is about allowing the Holy Spirit to empower us to do what God is calling us to do—arise and come to Him. He is the One who calls us to do it. And He is the One who enables us. Perhaps the most powerful Scripture passage to explain this process is found in a relatively obscure section of the Bible, the little Old Testament book of Micah:

> "Do not gloat over me, my enemy! Though I have fallen, I will rise. Though I sit in darkness, the Lord will be my light. Because I have sinned against him, I will bear the Lord's wrath, until he pleads my case

and upholds my cause. He will bring me out into the
light; I will see his righteousness" (Micah 7:8–9).

The essence of what the prophet is saying is that when a fallen
believer arises, it is never in his own strength. It is God in His
grace who enables the believer to rise. It is God who brings the
believer back into the light. This powerful passage illustrates the
incomprehensible nature of grace. The very God whom we have
offended is the One who pleads our cause and restores us to right
standing with Him!

As difficult as it may seem when we are lying in the filth of the
pigpen, that first step back toward God is the most significant we can
ever take. It is the beginning of a whole new journey that can take us
not only to forgiveness, but to restoration as sons and daughters of
our heavenly Father. This first step can lead us to destinations where
God can actually use us again for His glory. The first step always
leads to a next step.

And that can be the most challenging step of all.

Who am I?

Moses had seen some strange things in his forty years on the
Sinai Peninsula. But he had never seen anything to top that burning
bush. That talked. His encounter with the Great I AM of Israel that
day in the desert would forever change the course of Moses's life, as
well as all human history.

Moses had a history, too. Forty years earlier, he had been a
favored son in the palace of the Egyptian pharaoh. The king's
daughter had rescued him from the river as a baby and had raised
him as her own. But Moses knew he was not an Egyptian. He was
a Jew. One of God's chosen people. In fact, in the deepest places of
his soul, Moses knew he was chosen for even more.

One day, Moses secretly spied an Egyptian mistreating one
of the Hebrew slaves. In his anger, Moses struck and killed the
Egyptian. Suddenly, this prince of Egypt was a wanted man. Moses

fled from the face of Pharaoh and the Egyptian authorities and started a new life in the land of Midian. Actually, he fled from much more than that. He fled from everything he had once dreamed he might do and become.

Forty years later, God spoke to Moses from a burning bush on the backside of the desert. Moses would never forget those first words he heard as he debated whether or not to approach:

"Take off your sandals. For the place where you are standing is holy ground" (Exodus 3:5)

Moses was terrified. But something had given him the strength to move closer. He was certain these would be the hardest steps he would ever make. He would be mistaken.

The Lord told Moses that he was God's chosen man to free the Jews from their slavery and lead them out of Egypt. Moses' stunned response was predictable, if not typical:

"Who am I to lead the people?" (Exodus 3:11 NLT).

Rich: During the weeks after my meeting with CH, I prayed a lot that God would somehow give me the courage to try what I thought He was calling me to do. But the voice in my head was relentless. "Who do you think you are? You can't lead a high school Bible study after the life you've lived and the things you've done. Not one that would amount to anything anyway." I battled that voice with everything my spirit could muster. Finally, I just had to lean on God and trust Him to enable me.

One Saturday night, I shared the idea for a Bible study with the captain of the football team. Russell was a strapping, raw-boned, country boy with a humility that was rare for someone in his position. He was also the greatest leader I ever saw in a high school student. He said he really thought the guys would be hungry for something like that. We decided we would give it a shot. The following Thursday night, we would gather at my house and just see what the Lord had in store. That night, CH, three other guys, and I were sitting at my house, wondering if this was all it was going to be. Suddenly, in walked Russell with six guys trailing behind him. One of the guys there was Joe Harrell, a charismatic star running back that had transferred in from another state for his senior season. Joe had a tumultuous background, but he had a great heart. That night, Thursday Night Talk, or TNT, was born. God moved in the lives of Joe, Russell, and other student leaders, and within two months, over a hundred high school guys were gathering every week to hear biblical truth and to pour out their hearts to God and each other. Wounds were healed, pain was released, barriers were broken, and souls were saved. It remains to this day the single most spontaneous, miraculous work of God I have ever been a part of. And the greatest miracle of all was that He was using a broken vessel like me.

Rich's experience only serves to illustrate a timeless reality: God uses sinners. He has no other option. We are all broken vessels, flawed in some way or another. Some of us have more glaring blemishes than others. But the infallible God of heaven and earth is not limited by our imperfections. In fact, He uses them to display His amazing grace and mercy and to bring greater glory to His name. As the apostle Paul wrote:

"But God chose the foolish things of the world to shame the wise; God chose the weak things of the world to shame the strong. God chose the lowly things of this world and the despised things— and the things that are not—to nullify the things that are, so that no one may boast before him" (1 Corinthians 1:27–29).

No one can boast before God. The truth is, God made sure they couldn't by working through people with all sorts of weaknesses so that His strength might be obvious to everyone and His name might be glorified.

Everything God does brings glory to Him. That is not arrogant. If we did everything for our own glory, that would be arrogant and self-centered because we are neither worthy nor deserving of such glory. But for God to do so is perfectly appropriate because He is absolutely worthy and deserving of it. In fact, for God to glorify anything but Himself would be inappropriate and detrimental. The world and the universe are best served when their Creator is most glorified.

And His glory often shines brightest through the cracks of a broken vessel.

Wes: On the first day of December, I got up the courage to call Rich. I hadn't talked with him since getting the letter, but I knew he would treat me with grace, and he absolutely did. I was too scared to bring up the subject of moving in. I just told him I was tired of the life I had been living and knew I needed to change. I also told him how much I needed to get out of the place where I was living. I asked him if we could meet for lunch, and we agreed to meet a couple of days later. Maybe then I would be able to ask. I had no idea, but God was one step ahead of me. Seems like He always is.

Rich: I must admit that I was pretty floored when I heard Wesley's voice on the phone. After our conversation, I knew he was going to be looking for a place to live. I also knew this was an issue I was really going to have to commit to prayer. Could I possibly trust this guy who had been living a life that was immersed in so much sin and who had a child out of wedlock? What else was left over from his lifestyle? What if he was on drugs? What if he was running from something? What if he wasn't really serious? I had already determined that my new home was going to be a place of godliness, where people were passionately following Christ and sharpening each other spiritually. But I had also asked the Lord to make it a place of healing, restoration, and grace. I prayed that God would give me a peace about letting Wes live there. Within twenty-four hours, God clearly answered my prayer, and I know to this day letting Wes move in was one of the best decisions I ever made.

Wes: After I moved into Rich's house, I not only had a place where I knew I would receive grace and acceptance, but I would also have the accountability that had been so lacking in my life before. Rich explained that while I was an adult and he wasn't keeping any attendance charts, going to church would not be optional if I lived in his house. It was exactly what I needed because going back and facing so many people I thought I had let down was not going to be easy. (It actually turned out to be easier than I thought.) Although I was still deeply wounded by the sin of my past, I had finally found a place of healing and a spiritual family to help me do it.

Brothers in arms

There is simply no substitute for the brotherhood we have with other believers. Even Moses did not lead the Israelites out of Egypt alone. His brother Aaron was by his side. For any broken believer to properly heal, the encouragement of brothers and sisters in Christ is an essential medicine.

When Jesus predicted Simon Peter's denial, he told Peter that he would not only fall, he would repent and return to the Lord. The instruction Jesus gave him with regard to this time of restoration was simply this: "Strengthen your brothers" (Luke 22:32).

Jesus knew that in the aftermath of his crucifixion, not just Peter but all His disciples would be weak and frightened. And the Lord knew during that critical time they would desperately need God's sustaining presence and grace. But they would need something else as well:

They would need each other.

Rich: As great as the TNT experience was for me, I knew it was nowhere near my final step. It was only the beginning. I needed to re-establish fellowship with my church family and my pastor. But I was ashamed and scared. I had let them all down so badly, especially Rocky. It was bad enough that I had dishonored the office of deacon. Rocky had actually let me fill the pulpit. I just could not imagine how I could go back, let alone really be used again. Merely showing up at church was not difficult. I could do that without really engaging, and that is exactly what I did for a while. But then one night after the service, an old friend approached me. Mark and I had coached baseball together back in our younger days. His story was much like mine except that he had long since been on the road to recovery and restoration. He was now a deacon. "Rich," he told me, "You need to get back in the game, man. I know you feel like you've lost a lot of credibility around here, but I want you to know you can build it back. And it won't take nearly as long as you think it will." I don't know if Mark remembers those words, but I never forgot them. They spurred me on in some really challenging and discouraging times. I can't say enough about what CH meant to me either. I don't know what I would have done without brothers like those guys.

The stories couldn't possibly be true. The group of believers gathered that night knew the grace of Christ was powerful and far-reaching. But what they had heard recently had to be a false rumor. Yes, God could save anyone. But not this guy. Not someone whose very passion in life was to seek out, torture, and murder His followers. Not Saul.

They had heard tales of how Saul had seen the Lord in a vision and had been gloriously saved from his bloodthirsty lifestyle. But even if the stories were true, what if it was just a charade? It would be just like Saul to try to infiltrate their ranks and then betray them to the Jewish authorities. No, this was one they just couldn't buy.

Not on the word of a Christian-hating Pharisee. They would need more compelling evidence than that.

Suddenly, their discussion was interrupted by a knock at the door. It was Barnabas. Their spirits immediately lifted. They had been expecting him, but it was always such a joy to be in his presence. He was truly the son of encouragement. He had brought a guest, though they couldn't see the man's face.

"Greetings, all!" said Barnabas, as his companion stepped into the light. A collective gasp rose from the group when he lifted his face.

"This is our brother, Saul," Barnabas announced. "He has seen the Lord. And he now fearlessly preaches His Name."

The encouraging words of a brother or sister in Christ can often be the key that unlocks the flow of grace in our lives. And it is a powerful flow.

From both sides of the cross.

Questions to consider:

Is there a particular step you need to take in order to rediscover your God-given purpose?

Who and where are the specific brothers or sisters in Christ you need to deliberately connect with?

Truth to embrace:

God's plan for you has not been nullified by your mistakes.

"Then Peter stood up with the eleven, raised his voice and addressed the crowd" (Acts 2:14).

There is no substitute for the support of other believers.

"A friend loves at all times, and a brother is born for a time of adversity" (Proverbs 17:17).

There are brothers and sisters in Christ waiting to encourage you.

"Keep on loving one another as brothers and sisters" (Hebrews 13:1).

Chapter 9

The Other Side of Grace

> "If we confess our sins, he is faithful and just and will forgive us our sins and purify us from all unrighteousness" (1 John 1:9).

Grace is truly a wonderful thing. It is only by the unmerited favor and undeserved mercy of God that any sinner could ever be made right with Him. We are saved by grace and grace is the very source of our relationship with God. But grace is not just for unredeemed sinners. There is another side of grace that is especially for Christians.

Christians who are also sinners.

Grace for forgiveness

No one understood grace better than David. The shepherd boy who became a king was a man after God's own heart. He is the most vivid example we have of an Old Testament believer. And no believer ever made a bigger mess of his life than King David. But David had great faith that the same grace that introduced him to God as a shepherd boy would introduce him to God's forgiveness as a king.

It had been nearly a year since his adulterous encounter with Bathsheba. That fateful night led David down a path that was almost certain to end with his destruction. And it would have, had it not been for one faithful servant of God. Nathan the prophet had come to David one evening and boldly confronted him with the grievous sin the king had been trying to conceal. And Nathan did not spare the details.

"Why did you despise the word of the Lord by doing what is evil in his eyes? You struck down Uriah the Hittite with the sword and took his wife to be your own. You killed him with the sword of the Ammonites" (2 Samuel 12:9).

With one fell swoop, the king's cover was blown. His sin was not only exposed to himself and to Nathan—it had been evident to God all along. David could no longer fight the guilt. No doubt exhausted from constantly trying to cover his tracks, he confessed his sin to the Lord and to Nathan. The conversation that followed was difficult but necessary. Nathan outlined the inevitable consequences of David's actions. They would be extensive.

Something else would be extensive as well. God's forgiveness. David knew that even for the king, God's penalty for adultery and murder was death. Such a sin was particularly heinous for someone who should have known better. But the Lord spared David's life. This display of mercy was amazing. Grace always is. In the aftermath of such undeserved forgiveness, David journaled his thoughts in a poetic verse that would later become known to history as Psalm 51. Its opening verses reveal the heart of a truly broken believer:

"Have mercy on me, O God, according to your unfailing love; according to your great compassion, blot out my transgressions. Wash away all my iniquity and cleanse me from my sin" (Psalm 51:1–2).

David's relationship with God did not begin that night when he confessed his sin before Nathan. David had known the Lord since he tended sheep in his father's pastures as a youth. He was familiar with the greatness of God's mercy toward His children. But he also knew something even more powerful. David was confident that the flow of God's mercy sprang from a continuous fountain of grace that flowed to cleanse His children of all sin.

Past, present, and future.

Rich: When I began my journey back to the Lord, the first challenge I faced was placing my faith in the truth that God really did have grace to forgive a broken Christian. I was not coming to him as one who was lost, blind, and ignorant of the truth. I came as one who was already His and who should have known better than to do the things I had done. But after searching the Scriptures, I came across 1 John 1:9, which says, "If we confess our sins, he is faithful and just and will forgive us our sins and purify us from all unrighteousness." John's epistle was not written to unsaved people. It was written to believers. I knew that on the authority of His Word, God said He would forgive my sin. All of it. And I also knew that God could never deny His Word. I'm not saying it wasn't a battle. I can't begin to tell you how many times I have repeated 1 John 1:9 over and over in my head. It's amazing to think about, but I know from my own experience that there are a lot of believers that remain paralyzed because they just can't accept this truth.

It is indeed a paralyzing and debilitating proposition for a Christian to live under guilt. But God never intended for a believer to live that way. As John wrote and as David experienced firsthand, God's grace for forgiveness does not stop at the moment of our salvation. In fact, the very opposite is true. We only begin to experience grace when we become a Christian. Its abiding presence in our lives is there to continually deliver us from sin's guilt.

And from the wounds that often linger.

Grace for healing

For a Christian, being forgiven is a judicial fact. Christians are forgiven. When a person comes to Christ, all of his past life and deeds are wiped away and he is declared righteous before God. But grace does not stop there. Grace follows a believer for the rest of his days, ready to offer not only forgiveness from the past, but healing from its effects.

Effects that can otherwise be devastating.

Wes: Moving into the spare room at Rich's house was the best thing I could have possibly done in my situation. I knew God had forgiven me, but there was so much junk I was walking away from and a lot of damage in my life. I badly needed a place to heal. The grace I experienced, especially during those first couple of months, was incredible. Just having a place where I could sit in the presence of God was huge. It was so unlike the place I had been living. I was able to engage in helpful conversations with Rich and other believers or sometimes just be alone with God away from all the distractions. I know I could never have made the recovery I experienced without this time of healing in my life. Sure, I had desires to jump in and be used by God, but I knew I wasn't strong enough to do that yet. It was kind of like recovering from an injury or an illness. I needed time and a lot of grace to become healthy again. God was faithful to provide it.

The aftermath of a spiritual train wreck requires a sizable cleanup effort. Forgiveness is wonderful, but it doesn't clean up the wreckage. Or heal all the injuries. The spiritual wounds can often be deep and painful. As David penned the words of Psalm 51, he clearly had not only forgiveness in mind, but healing as well.

"Create in me a pure heart, O God, and renew a steadfast spirit within me" (Psalm 51:10).

King David trusted in God's faithfulness absolutely. He knew, on the word of Nathan the prophet, that God had heard his confession and forgiven his sin. But David also knew that forgiveness was not all he needed. He needed to be healed. The damage of David's sin would be extensive and far-reaching. But there was no doubt where the deepest wounds had been inflicted: in David's heart.

The heart is a powerful thing. It can cause people to do things they never thought themselves capable of. The heart is the most mysterious aspect of the human makeup. The Bible speaks of its ability to control, manipulate, and even blind us to the truth.

"The heart is deceitful above all things, and desperately wicked: who can know it?" (Jeremiah 17:9 NKJV).

As David faced the chaos and strife that would define his family in the years that followed his adulterous affair, his biggest problem was not the consequences of his sin. His biggest problem was inside of himself. His wicked heart needed to be healed. When David prayed for God to create in him a clean heart and to renew in him a steadfast spirit, he was echoing the cries of countless believers throughout the centuries:

The cry for a brand-new start.

Rich: Once I learned to embrace God's forgiveness for my sin, I began to focus my heart toward making a fresh start in my journey with Him. Through His amazing grace, I was able to kick my prescription drug habit in about two weeks. I do not by any means intend to suggest it was easy. I had tried to quit and failed many times. But this time, I put all my trust in God's grace, and He saw me through to victory. Since then, I have seen God miraculously deliver others from similar drug habits. I know without a shadow of a doubt that the power of Christ's supernatural grace really can heal us from addiction.

Feeling clean and forgiven again was great, but there was a tremendous amount of healing that had to take place within me, especially for what I had done to my mind. James Robison has said, "Pornography is a tattoo on the brain."[1] He is absolutely right. I had fed my mind so much poison during the preceding years that I was going to have to trust God for the grace to heal my thought processes. There was no way I could serve the Lord without significant healing from the damage inflicted by such demeaning images. When a person recovers from a pornography addiction, one of the first realities that hits home is that the people in those images are not computer graphics. They are flesh-and-blood people, created in the image of God. So I began to ask God to enable me to look at every person—regardless of age or gender—as a precious soul for whom Christ died; a special creation with whom God desires a special relationship. Over time, grace used this perspective to make all the difference.

The other issue was the shame. No sin has the power to shame us like sexual sin. Where the Enemy keeps a lot of men in bondage to pornography and sexual immorality is by shaming them into being afraid to confide in anyone about their struggle. God finally gave me the courage to confess my problem to some close brothers in Christ. I was amazed to find that many of them related to my struggle in a very personal way. The powerful deception that many men tragically believe is that freedom from sexual sin is impossible. I am living proof that such a belief is nothing more than a lie from the Enemy. Freedom is not only possible, it is the express will of God for your life. My advice to anyone trapped in a battle with pornography or some other addiction is to find a godly brother or sister in Christ and confess your struggle to them. You may be dealing with some things that don't need to be confessed publicly or to someone of the opposite sex, but that is not an excuse to keep your problem a secret. It was only when I started to build some accountability relationships into my life that God's amazing grace began the process of healing me from my addictions. I finally felt like I had a chance at a new beginning.

Grace for restoration

Forgiveness generally has to do with things that are already done. Healing is about being strengthened to face the challenges of each day. Restoration, however, is a much more forward-looking proposition. You might even say it like this: Forgiveness is grace for the past, healing is grace for the present, and restoration is grace for the future.

When a wayward believer returns to the Lord, the first and foremost issue he faces is understanding that God has forgiven him. Once he has embraced God's mercy, he must go through a period of healing from the wounds his detour has inflicted. But when the healing process reaches a certain point, a true believer begins to look to Christ for restoration to his proper place in the Father's house.

Wes: The first few months after I came back to the Lord were a battle. Living at Rich's house had given me a place to heal and grow, but I still faced huge challenges. Not only was I periodically tempted by people and things from my old life, but I was also faced with attacks of doubt that I would ever be used by God again. I had gone to the Passion 2011 Conference for college students in January, and God had really spoken to my heart that I had a story to tell and something to offer in His kingdom. I asked CH, who was still the youth pastor at my church, if I could sit in on a small group and offer encouraging words to the students. I began to build relationships with some of the high school guys that spring. By the time summer came, I was able to go to camp with the student ministry. Several years earlier, Chad, Dane, and I had been small group leaders at the same camp for sixth-grade boys. Those same boys who I had once helped disciple were now seniors. On the last night, I really felt God's Spirit calling me to commit the rest of my life to being a godly man. I went down to the altar to pray, and within seconds, I was engulfed by the entire group of senior guys. I had completely missed being around to watch them grow up spiritually, yet here we all were, weeping and embracing as I poured out my heart to God. Some of them told me later what an impact my testimony had on their lives. It was one of the most awesome moments of grace I have ever experienced. I began to feel like my life mattered again, and that I might really have a future as a servant in the kingdom of God.

Of all the challenges that face a Christ-follower recovering from a spiritual fall, the greatest is believing that God can actually restore him to his original place in the kingdom. There is just something in our fallen minds that has a hard time accepting the idea that we won't be spiritually handicapped for the rest of our days. Our natural tendency is to assume that God puts believers who have strayed in some sub-category of kingdom servants who have "limitations."

Nothing could be further from the truth.

The consequences of sin are real. There is no mistaking that. But broken believers returning to the Lord can hope not only in God's forgiveness and healing, but also in the reality that He can and will restore them to the full benefits of their salvation. David was well aware of God's desire and willingness to do this when he wrote Psalm 51:

"Restore to me the joy of your salvation and grant me a willing spirit, to sustain me. Then I will teach transgressors your ways, so that sinners will turn back to you" (Psalm 51:12–13).

Rich: As great as it was to be back in fellowship with God and my church family, I knew I would never again walk in the fullness of joy until I was at the place where God could effectively use me. I was well aware of the gifts He had placed in me many years earlier, and I also knew His calling on my life to preach His Word. Even with everything that had happened in my life, it was my firm belief that those gifts and that calling were still very much alive. I began to seek out Scripture passages that spoke of God's power to restore His people, and I found many to encourage me. I had always thought grace was just about having your sins forgiven or being "saved." But as I began to experience God's emotional and mental healing, I started to see a dimension of grace I never knew existed. God really did have more than enough grace to restore me and give me opportunities in the future that I had wasted in the past. I know it doesn't sound fair that God would give someone who had been so irresponsible a second chance at their calling, but I truly believe that is the amazing aspect of grace that can set a lot of paralyzed believers free. God really is our heavenly Father, and He wants to fully restore us to our place and privilege as beloved sons and daughters.

In Psalm 51:12, David spoke of the "joy of your salvation." In the very next verse, he talked about teaching transgressors the ways of God. For many Christians, some of the greatest joys they ever experience as God's children are the opportunities they have to use their gifts in ministering to others. Restoration to the fullness of our sonship and usefulness is exactly what God desires when we return to Him. This principle could not be illustrated more clearly than in the father's response to the return of the Prodigal Son.

"But the father said to his servants, 'Quick! Bring the best robe and put it on him. Put a ring on his finger and sandals on his feet. Bring the fattened calf and kill it. Let's have a feast and celebrate. For this son of mine was dead and is alive again; he was lost and is found.' So they began to celebrate" (Luke 15:22–24).

The father in the story restored all the powers, privileges, gifts, and opportunities of full sonship to the Prodigal. To believe that God would not restore these gifts or opportunities to a repentant believer is to fundamentally misunderstand grace.

Yet, there are those in the very body of Christ who suffer from this misunderstanding. Some of these well-meaning brothers and sisters are convinced that when a Christian makes a mess of his life, he can only return to the Lord on perpetual probation. He can never be fully restored to usefulness in the kingdom. The Prodigal Son had just such a brother in his own life.

"The older brother became angry and refused to go in. So his father went out and pleaded with him. But he answered his father, 'Look! All these years I've been slaving for you and never disobeyed your orders. Yet you never gave me even a young goat so I could celebrate with my friends. But when this son of yours who has squandered your property with prostitutes comes home, you kill the fattened calf for him!' "(Luke 15:28–30).

The reaction of the self-righteous older son to the father's restoration of the Prodigal is unfortunately not an uncommon one. Even against the backdrop of the amazing, healing, and restoring grace of God in the life of a returning believer, there will inevitably be juxtaposed another presence—a presence that offers the next great challenge in the long journey home.

The presence of an enemy.

Questions to consider:

Do you believe without question or doubt that God is willing to forgive all your sin—even the ones committed after you came to Christ?

Do you really believe that God wants to restore you to the fullness of your position as His son or daughter?

Truth to embrace:

God never condemns His born-again children.

"Therefore, there is now no condemnation for those who are in Christ Jesus" (Romans 8:1).

We are completely forgiven through the blood of Christ.

"In him we have redemption through his blood, the forgiveness of sins, in accordance with the riches of God's grace" (Ephesians 1:7).

God wants us to be fully functional sons and daughters.

"So you have not received a spirit that makes you fearful slaves. Instead, you received God's Spirit when he adopted you as his own children. Now we call him, 'Abba, Father'" (Romans 8:15 NLT).

Chapter 10

Silencing the Accuser

The return of a prodigal is a glorious thing. The forgiveness, healing,
and restoration a wayward child receives when he comes home to
the Father is an unforgettable experience. But for most believers who
have strayed, the joy of restored fellowship with God is almost always
challenged in the inevitable battle that follows.

The same devil that lurks in the shadows ready to take down
unsuspecting Christians also stands ready to accuse those same
believers after they have returned to the Lord. His attacks are
strategic and calculated.

And relentless.

*Rich: Among the greatest challenges I faced in the process of
being restored to service in God's kingdom were what I would
call satanic attacks. My life experience has left no doubt in my
mind that we have a real, personal, spiritual enemy. The closer*

I moved to full restoration as a servant of God, the stronger the Enemy's opposition became. For me, the most common attacks were mental. Thoughts would bombard my mind like "Who do think you are, trying to help others spiritually?" Or, "God could never use someone with a past like yours." I've heard some teachers say the Devil can't read your thoughts. That may be true, but that doesn't mean he can't stimulate them. A TV commercial here, an innocent comment there, a strategically placed article in the news, I'm not sure exactly how his mental assaults work, but I do know they happen. He may not be able to read minds, but he can definitely press our mental buttons. And he knows exactly which buttons to press. If we are going to fight him successfully, we have to fight for our minds.

Know the truth

Jesus made a very famous and often quoted statement that is recorded in the eighth chapter of the gospel of John:

"The truth shall set you free."

These immortal words from our immortal Savior have become one of the most iconic statements He ever uttered. They have been applied to situations in virtually every arena of life, both religious and secular. Unfortunately, they are but a fragment of what Jesus actually said in the passage from which they have been lifted. The entire quote reads like this:

"So Jesus was saying to those Jews who had believed Him, 'If you continue in My word, then you are truly disciples of Mine; and you will know the truth, and the truth will make you free' " (John 8:31–32 NASB).

Understanding the context in which Jesus spoke these words makes all the difference for a child of God locked in mortal combat with the Devil. It isn't just any "truth" that sets people free. It is the Word of God.

Jesus told His followers that in order to be set free by the truth, they had to know the truth. And as Jesus made clear, the only way to know the truth in this liberating way is to continue in His Word.

The Bible is the Word of God and is absolute, infallible truth. The apostle Paul wrote that it is the only offensive weapon the believer possesses with which to fight off the attacks of the Enemy.

"Take the helmet of salvation and the sword of the Spirit, which is the word of God" (Ephesians 6:17).

It is important that we note the original language of this verse. The Greek word that is translated "word of God" in Ephesians 6:17 is the word rhema. It literally means "a particular word from God." Notice that Paul did not use the word logos, which commonly refers to the whole Bible. This is a significant point because as believers we do not fight Satan with a Bible. We fight him with specific truth (rhema) from the Bible.

The Bible is all true. In fact, some have suggested it is true from the table of contents to the maps of the Holy Land. But merely believing in its veracity will not empower us if we do not know what it says. If we do not read, memorize, and meditate on the rhema of the logos, we make ourselves easy targets for the Enemy's lies. We must know the Word of God.

And that means knowing the God of the Word.

The truth about God

When the Enemy attacks our minds, one of his primary targets is our concept of God. This is a strategy that aims at the very center of how we view life itself. It could certainly be argued that the single most important thing about a person is what he thinks about God. What we believe about our heavenly Father often shapes what we believe about life.

Especially when life becomes a train wreck.

Wes: The biggest obstacles I faced in coming back from my dark journey were the lies that kept attacking my mind. Satan was determined to keep me in the cell where he had imprisoned me for nearly five years. Some of the biggest lies I encountered were about God's mercy. The Devil wanted to convince me that God would never use someone with a track record like mine. Thoughts and fears that I would never be able to live the life of a godly man presented an almost constant challenge for me at first. I spent more than a few sleepless nights, wondering if I would ever really live in His blessing again. It was not until I made a life-changing decision that I began to have genuine victory. I made up my mind to get in the Word and saturate my thoughts with God's truth. I started reading the Bible and other Christian books every day. And not just reading, but really meditating on God's truth. Don't get me wrong— it definitely was not an easy discipline to start, but in the end it made all the difference.

There is only one counterattack weapon against an onslaught of the Devil's lies—and that is the truth of God's Word. For every lie the Enemy tries to tell us about God, there is a truth that is able to cast it down. The only hope a believer has against such attacks is to know and saturate his mind with the truth of God.

And the truth about God.

The story of the Prodigal Son makes absolutely clear the character of our Father in heaven. He is loving, kind, and merciful. He desires fellowship with His children, even more than we desire it with Him. It is crucial for us to remember that reconciliation was so important to God that He was willing to pay the ultimate price to have us for Himself. In his second letter to the Corinthian believers, Paul talked about the true nature and desire of God toward His children:

"God was reconciling the world to himself in Christ, not counting people's sins against them. And he has committed to us the message of reconciliation" (2 Corinthians 5:19).

Did you catch that, believer? God does not count our sins against us! This is the most glorious truth in the universe and the powerful truth about our Father that the Devil does not want us to know. God is not a dreadful taskmaster who desires to punish His wayward children or to relegate us to the status of unworthy slaves when we fail. God is a reconciler! He is a gracious father who desires nothing less for prodigals than full restoration to our positions in His family.

Positions which the Enemy always seeks to dispute.

The truth about us

If there is anything as important about us as our view of God, it is most certainly our view of ourselves. Running parallel with Satan's attempts to distort our image of our Father is often just as powerful an assault on our image of ourselves. The Devil doesn't just attack who Christ is. He attacks who we are in Christ.

For wounded believers, there are few challenges that rise to the level of the Enemy's assault on our spiritual identity. Most of us can eventually come to terms with what the Bible says about God. But it is a different matter entirely to embrace what the Bible says about us.

Especially when we know all the dirt.

Rich: I could deal with the Devil's attacks on the truth about God. I had always been grounded in my beliefs about the person and character of God and the redeeming power of Jesus. But a far greater challenge was reclaiming what I knew to be the biblical truth about myself. I already knew what the Bible said. I had read many of its passages dozens of times. It said I was a son of God, completely forgiven and all that. But my life experience painted a very different picture. I knew the severity of the sin I had lived in. I was there when it happened. For quite some time, I allowed it to hinder me in my return to effectively serving God. Eventually, it took a serious commitment to the Word of God to propel me to the next level. I had to literally fast from secular activities and immerse myself in the teaching of the Bible.

Within about six weeks of saturating my mind with the Word, I found myself becoming a new man. The Word of God had awakened me to the powerful truths that every believer should walk in. I was thinking clearly again about who I was and what was available to me as a child of God. My newfound passion for the Word awakened me to a dynamic that turned out to be a game-changer for me. I learned to see spiritual battle not as a fight to avoid negative consequences, but as an opportunity to reap great rewards. It was a revolutionary thought to me!

There really is incredible spiritual reward for the believer who is willing to fight! It was one of the most inspiring times of my life, and it developed permanent habits in me that are there to this day. God told us that the key to transformation is the renewing of our minds. I am living proof of that reality.

The Bible is no ordinary book. It is the living, supernatural Word of God. It has the ability to unleash the power of God in the life of a child of God. For a believer who has returned to the Lord, the Devil will try every means he can to block the flow of that power. But even the mighty Prince of Darkness is no match for the eternal truth of God's Word about Christians.

Truths such as these:

> You are sons and daughters of the Most High God (Romans 8:16).

> You are completely forgiven (1 John 1:9).

> You are the righteousness of God in Christ (2 Corinthians 5:21).

You are blessed with every spiritual blessing (Ephesians 1:3).

You have been given the victory through the Lord Jesus Christ (1 Corinthians 15:57).

You are born of incorruptible seed (1 Peter 1:23).

You are a joint heir with Christ of everything God owns (Romans 8:17).

The volume of truth the Bible declares over believers is more than enough to disarm the Enemy of his most powerful weapons against us. But reading words on a page is not enough to truly transform us into the victorious vessels we are redeemed to be. Believers must be willing to go to a level that involves more than just reading the Bible. Because living in the power of God's Word is not merely a habit.

It is a mindset.

Set your mind

The twelfth chapter of the book of Romans is one of the greatest "how to" passages on living the Christian life in the entire Bible. In it, Paul goes into great specifics about how we should live and how we should treat others. He also gives us a great reason why we should live this way—it is an act of worship.

"Therefore, I urge you, brothers and sisters, in view of God's mercy, to offer your bodies as a living sacrifice, holy and pleasing to God—this is your true and proper worship" (Romans 12:1).

But in the second verse, the apostle tells believers the great secret to living the way Christ commands us to live:

We must renew our minds.

Wes: When I first moved into Rich's house, I was in recovery mode. I was tired of my old life and ready to be free from it. But I really didn't have much hunger for the things I knew I needed in order to change my life. That's when I began to force-

feed myself the Word. I literally made myself read the Bible and other books by Christian authors every night. Being a college-aged guy, I had a lot of potential distractions to reading. Video games were a big one. After about two months of battling the temptation not to read, I decided to take drastic measures. I gave Rich the power cord to my game system and told him to hide it for thirty days. It was the beginning of the most major transformation of my life. Slowly but surely, my hunger for the Word started coming back, and I began thinking differently about God, myself, and my future. I learned that the mind is an incredibly powerful thing, and the most important key to living the life Christ calls us to.

The battle Wes found himself in with his video games was really the same one he had been in for five years. He was just finally learning how to fight it. Any Christian is going to face essentially the same thing from the world: a well-orchestrated attempt to press them into its mold. That is the essence of Romans 12:2.

"Do not conform to the pattern of this world, but be transformed by the renewing of your mind. Then you will be able to test and approve what God's will is—his good, pleasing and perfect will" (Romans 12:2).

The translated word for conform in this verse is the Greek word suschematizo. It literally means to make something appear to be something it is not. The idea is similar to that of a cookie cutter. You can make a cookie look pretty much like anything you want—a star or a kitten or a Christmas tree—if you have the right mold. But it really isn't any of those things. In its essential internal makeup, it is still a cookie.

The same thing happens when a Christian allows the secular culture of the world to be his primary influence. The world will incessantly try to "cookie cut" that believer into something that no longer looks like a child of God. Like Wes and Rich experienced, he may be a Christian on the inside, but his appearance will be anything but Christlike.

But as Paul reminds us in Romans 12:2, there is a solution to the madness. The way to keep from being conformed by the world's cookie cutter is to be transformed by the renewing of your mind. The word transformed in the Greek is metamorphoo. It means to be changed from the inside out. Its root word is morphe, which refers to the essential being of something. Being transformed in this sense means being changed not merely in what we look like, but in who we are as well.

Renewing the mind is an absolute necessity if a Christian is going to silence the voice of the Enemy and become who he is meant to be. That is what the Word of God will do for a believer. The power of a renewed mind will change him from the inside out into the new creation that he really is in Christ and will enable him to discover God's plan and purpose for his life.

And that is something truly wonderful.

Questions to consider:

What specific lies has the Enemy assaulted your mind with about God and about you?

What steps do you need to take to make the Word of God your primary focus?

Truth to embrace:

As believers, we have everything we need to protect us against the Enemy's attacks.

"Put on the full armor of God, so that you can take your stand against the devil's schemes" (Ephesians 6:11).

We must be mindful of the Enemy's schemes and always willing to stand and fight.

"Be alert and of sober mind. Your enemy the devil prowls around like a roaring lion looking for someone to devour. Resist him, standing firm in the faith" (1 Peter 5:8-9).

The Word of God overcomes every lie of the Devil.

"For the word of God is living and powerful, and sharper than any two-edged sword, piercing even to the division of soul and spirit, and of joints and marrow, and is a discerner of the thoughts and intents of the heart" (Hebrews 4:12 NKJV).

Section Four: The Masterpiece

> "For we are God's masterpiece. He has created us anew in Christ Jesus, so we can do the good things he planned for us long ago" (Ephesians 2:10 NLT).

Chapter 11

The Great Exchange

> "God made him who had no sin to be sin for us, so that in him we might become the righteousness of God"
> (2 Corinthians 5:21).

"Repent and be baptized, every one of you, in the name of Jesus Christ for the forgiveness of your sins!" (Acts 2:38).

The people of Jerusalem had never heard a preacher speak with such power. They had heard stories about the prophets of old proclaiming the word of the Lord. Many of them had even heard Jesus Himself preach. But from a man, they had never experienced a sermon like this one.

The preacher was so bold, so convicted of the truth he was proclaiming. It was as if the very fire of heaven was spewing forth from his mouth as he spoke the words that had captivated the crowd. So moved were the multitudes that some three thousand of them fell to their knees that very moment, repenting of their sins and confessing the lordship of Jesus of Nazareth. It was the birthday of the church.

The speaker that day in Jerusalem was Simon Peter, the son of John from the town of Capernaum in Galilee. But it was not Peter the fisherman who the crowds heard that morning. Neither was it Peter the fearful disciple who hid himself in the shadows one dark Thursday night scarcely two months before. This was someone much more than just Peter.

This was a Holy Spirit-filled apostle of the Lord Jesus Christ.

More than forgiven

The process by which a fallen believer is restored to fullness as a servant of Christ can be a difficult one for many people to grasp. The drastic transformation that took place in the life of Peter in the fifty days between Passover and Pentecost is no less challenging for the human mind to fathom. How, in such a relatively short time, could one go from cowering in the darkness, denying the name of Jesus, to boldly proclaiming that same name in broad daylight to the very same people? Such a question can only be answered by what happened in between.

The day after Peter's fireside denial outside the home of the high priest was the day that changed everything. For every person who would ever confess the name of Jesus, that Friday was the day that would alter the course of history. It was the day of the cross. And it was not merely the day we were forgiven. It was the day of the great exchange.

No verse of Scripture captures the magnitude of the cross quite like the theme verse of this chapter:

"For He made Him who knew no sin to be sin for us, that we might become the righteousness of God in Him" (2 Corinthians 5:21 NKJV).

Christ became sinful because of us. We became righteous because of Christ. The formula for the exchange was simple. The process of the exchange was painful. The power of the exchange is limitless.

Rich: My dark journey and subsequent return to the Lord was not just about being forgiven. It was so much more than that. It breaks my heart to see how many Christians think being forgiven is all there is to being in relationship with Jesus. It's like they have this "forgiveness card" in their pocket, and every time they screw up, they just pull out the card. They're going to heaven when they die because they are forgiven. It is shocking how many professing believers see their faith that way. One thing my experience has taught me is that grace is not merely about forgiveness! To look at it like that is just so far beneath what Christ did for us at the cross. I know that God has forgiven me of every sin I ever committed—accidentally, ignorantly, or on purpose. But the cross means so much more than that. Jesus didn't just forgive me. He didn't just take away my sin. He gave me the righteousness of God in return! I am the righteousness of God, in Christ! Embracing that reality has done far more than just enable me to lay my head down in peace at night. It has given me a reason to get up in the morning.

There simply is no higher reality, no greater reason to live than to know the awesome truth of 2 Corinthians 5:21. For a child of God, it is the most glorious truth in the universe. We are the righteousness of God.

This is a concept so far beyond anything our minds can comprehend that it almost sounds sacrilegious to explain it. When Christ went to the cross, he enabled us to exchange our old life for His new life, our filth for His holiness, our hopelessness for His glory. And our sin for His righteousness.

A righteousness that is as righteous as God.

Rich: It wasn't until several years after I had been restored to my walk with God that I came across a truth I had never thought about before. It was the idea that, based on 2 Corinthians 5:21, I was as righteous as God. When I first considered this concept,

I just sat there for a moment, stunned at such a thought. "How could that be?" my mind kept asking. "Me? As righteous as God?" It just didn't seem like a notion that should even be entertained. But the more I studied it, the more I began to see the majestic, incomprehensible truth of the passage. At the cross, Jesus took my sin—all of it—off of me forever. And in its place, he imputed to me His righteousness. And just how righteous is that righteousness? Well, I had no problem believing that Jesus was as righteous as God. And that could mean only one incredible thing. In the judicial eyes of heaven, I am as righteous as the Holy Almighty God of heaven and earth! That will do more than make you shout. That will take your breath away.

The double cure

There is an old hymn that illustrates perhaps better than any other the incomprehensible, double-barreled truth of the gospel. Its opening verse reads as follows:

"Rock of Ages, cleft for me,
Let me hide myself in Thee;
Let the water and the blood
From Thy wounded side which flowed,
Be of sin the double cure,
Save from wrath and make me pure." [1]

There really is a double cure offered by the gospel. Not only does the cross of Jesus save us from God's wrath, it also makes us pure and righteous, enabling us to live the life Christ saved us to live. We are not merely forgiven. We are made righteous.

No matter what we have done.

The emotions coursing through her body would have been enough to render most people unconscious. Yet in the midst of nearly coming undone, something was holding her together. Something she could not explain.

It had all happened so fast. With blinding speed, her privacy had been invaded, her shame put on display, her life placed in the hands of an angry mob. They had her, dead to rights. She was guilty. She knew it—and so did they. Surely the rabbi they had brought her to would agree that the only just penalty for her sin was death. All he had to do was give the word.

But it was a word that never came. As she stood with head bowed, unable to face her vicious accusers, the very Word Himself stepped in between. He spoke to the mob—something she could barely make out—as He kneeled to the ground and started to draw in the dirt. She braced herself for their attack. But one by one, her accusers began to walk away, until she stood alone face to face with the Son of God. His words to the crowd had escaped her. But she would never forget His words to her.

"Woman, where are those accusers of yours? Has no one condemned you?" (John 8:10 NKJV).

She could barely answer. "No one, Lord" (John 8:11 NKJV).

But although the mob had been dispersed, the adulteress was far from home free. She had been given a respite from those who were calling for her life. But she now stood at the mercy of the only One who had both the right and the power to take it.

Jesus's next words would echo through the corridors of her mind for the rest of her days.

"Neither do I condemn you; go now and leave your life of sin" (John 8:11).

In perhaps His most famous public display of grace, Jesus forgave the woman caught in adultery. In the face of a fanatical mob and a law that seemed to have no loopholes, the Son of God pulled the ultimate legal maneuver. He proved that the court in which the woman was being tried had no moral standing to convict her. He disarmed their vigilante justice by exposing their corruption. Then He did the unthinkable.

There in the city of Jerusalem, in the shadow of Calvary's hill, Jesus declared that the only court that could justly convict the woman would instead show mercy. That day, the Son of Man served notice to everyone what he had told a Pharisee one night in secret.

"For God did not send His Son into the world to condemn the world, but that the world through Him might be saved" (John 3:17 NKJV).

How could Jesus do such a thing? How could He seemingly ignore a clear Old Testament law by letting an adulteress go free? How could he make such an outlandish statement as to tell that same adulteress to leave her life of sin? Questions such as these can only be answered by one contingency:

The great exchange of the cross.

Jesus knew exactly where He was going when He encountered the lynch mob and their victim that day in Jerusalem. He was going to Golgotha. And on that hill, He would take the stones meant for the adulteress. The bruises she deserved would become His. He would be punished. She would be forgiven. He would wear the shackles of her sin. And she would go free.

But freedom and forgiveness were not all that Jesus offered the woman that day. When the Lord spoke the words, "Go, and leave your life of sin," He offered her much more than that. He offered her the righteousness of God.

This woman may have been the first person in history who was directly offered the great exchange of the new covenant. Her guilt for His forgiveness. Her sin for His righteousness. It was the great exchange. It was the double cure. She was not only saved from wrath. She was made pure.

Such an amazing reality is possible for those who belong to Christ because of all Jesus accomplished for us at the cross. He didn't just take our sin. He literally took our place. But Christ did even more than that at Calvary. He did not die merely to forgive us. He died for us so that He could live in us. Jesus wants to deliver us from a life of sin and self-indulgence; to not only grant us judicial righteousness, but to lift us to a higher level of living. He is our righteousness because He is our life.

A life that carries immense purpose.

Wes: It was several months after I came back to the Lord when I began to realize my journey was about more than just healing and forgiveness. As our pastor so often reminds us, God had rescued me because there was someone He wanted me to be and something He wanted me to do. Sharing my testimony with some of the high school and college guys at camp was a real awakening. It was like God catapulted my life into a new realm of purpose. I had known for some time that He wanted to use my story, but I lacked the confidence to really do anything because I just didn't know the Bible like I should. It wasn't until I got into the Word consistently that I began to see myself as I really was. I was not just a sinner saved by grace. I was God's masterpiece. He had uniquely and perfectly designed me for His purposes, and I was ready to start discovering them.

God's masterpiece. The language of Ephesians 2:10 contains some of the most powerfully descriptive words in the New Testament. In its declaration of who believers are in Christ, the passage uses the Greek word poeima. Although the English translations of the verse usually render the word as masterpiece or workmanship, its root meaning could not be more apparent.

We are God's poem.

Divine destination

Many people misunderstand grace. Even people who have professed faith in Jesus Christ often seem to miss the point of their salvation. They understand the concept of being forgiven. They are reasonably confident of the notion that they will spend eternity in heaven rather than hell. But that is sadly the extent of their Christianity. They never go to the next level.

Ephesians 2:10 is a "next level" kind of verse. Following perhaps the greatest passage on salvation in the entire Bible, the verse goes on to tell us what God wants us to do with His amazing grace.

"For we are His workmanship, created in Christ Jesus for good works, which God prepared beforehand that we should walk in them" (Ephesians 2:10 NKJV).

What a revolutionary concept! We aren't saved just to go to heaven or to walk around in a state of being forgiven. We are not created in Christ Jesus merely so we can join a church and eat potluck dinners. We are saved for much more than that.

We are saved for a divine purpose.

God has a unique and specific plan for every person who comes to faith in Jesus Christ. This plan is so specific, in fact, that the Bible says God prepared it beforehand. Imagine that! Even when you were living life in rebellion against God or perhaps were oblivious to Him, God was preparing something wonderful for you to do as His masterpiece.

Something only you could do.

Rich: It was not until I deliberately immersed myself in the Word of God that I began to realize I still had a calling. I knew God had called me to preach when I was in my late teens, but I also knew I had been a very irresponsible steward of His commission. Years of walking in darkness can have a debilitating effect, even on someone who is gifted to serve the kingdom. But after I returned to the Lord—and more specifically to His Word—I discovered that His call on my life had not been revoked. In fact, it couldn't be. I was the only person God had uniquely designed to fulfill my mission for the times, places, and people to which I would be sent.

The notion that no one else can fulfill your specific calling is troubling to some people. Their assertion is that such an idea somehow undermines the sovereignty of God. But if we are to believe Ephesians 2:10, it is that very same Sovereign God who has ordained a plan for each believer that no one else can duplicate. You are perfectly designed for the unique assignment God has planned for you. No one else is. Just you. And by receiving the great exchange Jesus offers, you can begin to pursue the life you were made for with all of your heart.

No matter who you are.

It was growing late, though no deeper into the night than many of these conversations by the fire had taken them. The twelve had once again been captivated by the depth of the Master's words. They had never heard such teaching. He spoke as one having authority; not like the ordinary teachers in the temple court. They sat mesmerized in His presence. No one even noticed the hooded figure lurking in the trees just beyond the camp. No one but Jesus.

One by one, the disciples took their leave of the circle and bedded down for the night. Finally, Jesus found Himself alone with the fire. But He knew He was not really alone. The cloaked intruder had stealthily made his way into the campsite and now stood close by as Jesus looked up.

"Come, friend," said the Lord with a kind wave.

Lifting his hood, the Pharisee approached. He seemed troubled.

"Rabbi," he spoke nervously. "I am Nicodemus. May I speak with you?"

A teacher of the law himself, Nicodemus had heard Jesus preach on numerous occasions. His messages were so unlike any Nicodemus had ever heard. The truth Jesus taught was deep and profound. The Pharisee's hope that night was to gain some insight into the source of the Master's wisdom. Perhaps Jesus could offer some explanation that would satisfy Nicodemus's curiosity. But in the conversation that followed, Nicodemus would learn that he needed much more than intellectual satisfaction.

He needed a whole new beginning.

Questions to consider:

Do you long to experience the kind of radical transformation we see in the life of the apostle Peter?

Has your Christian life been primarily about being forgiven or about pursuing a divine calling?

Truth to embrace:

Christ desires His followers to live radically changed lives.

"For he has rescued us from the dominion of darkness and brought us into the kingdom of the Son he loves" (Colossians 1:13).

God wants to make every believer more like His Son.

"And we all, who with unveiled faces contemplate the Lord's glory, are being transformed into his image with ever-increasing glory, which comes from the Lord, who is the Spirit" (2 Corinthians 3:18).

Grace is given so that we might be free to pursue our highest callings.

"You, my brothers and sisters, were called to be free. But do not use your freedom to indulge the flesh; rather, serve one another humbly in love" (Galatians 5:13).

Chapter 12

Born Again

Nicodemus, a Pharisee and member of the religious ruling class, had come to Jesus under cover of darkness with a burning question: How could a simple, itinerant preacher speak with such profound authority if He were not sent directly from God?

The Lord's response was as profound as the Pharisee's question.

"Jesus replied, 'Very truly I tell you, no one can see the kingdom of God unless they are born again' " (John 3:3).

As perplexing as the answer may have been for Nicodemus, being born again is a perfectly understandable concept to a child of God. We die to our flesh; we are born of His Spirit. We die to our old life; we are born into His new life. The verse that perhaps best captures this reality is found in Paul's second letter to the Corinthians.

"Therefore, if anyone is in Christ, he is a new creation; old things have passed away; behold, all things have become new" (2 Corinthians 5:17 NKJV).

In this verse, the apostle Paul makes a powerful declaration about the state of a born-again believer. And while the context of 2 Corinthians 5 is talking about a new Christian, the same reality applies to those believers who have returned from a journey into the darkness. This glorious process of healing and restoration feels a lot like coming to Christ for the very first time.

It's like being born again. Again.

A new beginning

Rich: I want to state for the record that I don't think I became a Christian when I returned to the Lord after my years of wandering. I continue to affirm that I belonged to Jesus even during my darkest days. Having said that, I will admit that coming back into fellowship with God after the life I had been living felt a whole lot like being born again. Not in a theological sense, but a very practical one. I think it feels that way for any believer who is rescued from a sinful lifestyle. It's like getting a "do-over" or a second chance at the life God made you for. I believe the reason the experience of restoration is so much like being born again for a Christian is precisely because of what the Bible says about one who is born of God. He simply cannot go on living in sin. A believer has already been born of the very seed of God into a new kind of existence that is not like the old, sinful life of the flesh. If not properly nourished, this seed of God may lie dormant for a season, but it will eventually spring to life. Even though the believer may fall or even stray for a period of time, he will ultimately return to who he is. For me, this return was every bit as sweet as when I first came to Christ. Maybe even sweeter.

For a number of believers, their return to the Lord as prodigal children is an even more powerful experience than their initial salvation. That is because many of these Christians lack the maturity to take the necessary steps to truly grow in their faith upon first coming to Christ. The absence of accountability partners coupled with their spiritual immaturity plunges them into a worldly lifestyle that is often worse than the one they experienced as unbelievers.

But when the grace of God brings these prodigal children home, many of them approach their second chance at a life of faith with far greater humility and wisdom than they did the first time. These new beginnings are powerful and can often produce incredible amounts of spiritual fruit.

And spiritual influence.

Wes: When I was in high school, I did all the stuff a Christian teenager was expected to do. But other than Dane, I'm not sure I ever really influenced anybody. Man, did that change after I came back to the Lord. It was unbelievable how many people God allowed me to impact almost immediately after He began to turn my life around. People who hadn't been to church or given much thought to spiritual things were suddenly sensitive to conversations about God. It was like He was using me as a doorway for others to come to Him. It really did feel like I was getting a second chance at opportunities I had wasted when I was younger.

Then a little over a year after I came back to the Lord, I had a really significant opportunity. I was able to share my testimony with a guy a few years younger than me. Matt was a college student who had been a strong Christ follower as a teenager. But after high school, his life had really gotten off track. His story was so much like mine, and it was amazing how God brought us together and used my testimony in Matt's life. Shortly after meeting him, his life was radically transformed and restored

by the same grace I had experienced. He is one of the closest
brothers in Christ I have now. I know exactly what Rich means
now when he talks about being a door-holder.

Wesley's story is not unique. In fact, it is God's will for every
believer who has lost his way. The Father wants to give every single
one of His wayward sons and daughters a new beginning; a spiritual
second wind. Through his relationship with Matt, Wes awakened
to his usefulness to the kingdom of God in a powerful way. His
experience illustrates God's desire for every prodigal to rediscover
the journey they were made to take.

And the people they were made to take it with.

A new family

One of the most challenging but absolutely essential elements
to a wounded believer's recovery is finding a family of believers with
which to surround himself. The encouragement and accountability
provided by such a support group are necessities to the process of
spiritual healing. But the challenge is not usually with finding your
new family. It is with leaving your old one. God issued just such a
challenge to the forefather of our faith.

"The Lord had said to Abram, 'Go from your country, your
people and your father's household to a land which I will show you'
" (Genesis 12:1).

God unequivocally told Abram (later called Abraham), that if he
was going to truly embrace the life God had for him, it was going to
be necessary to leave some old relationships and seek out some new
ones. It wasn't that Abram's family was necessarily made up of bad
people. But they represented for Abram something every believer
must ultimately be willing to leave behind:

A comfort zone.

Wes: A few months into my recovery, I found myself starting
to plateau spiritually. It wasn't that I had slipped back into

*anything really bad, but I just stopped growing. At least, I
wasn't growing at the rate I knew I needed to. My problem was
simple, and it was painfully obvious to me. I was still hanging
out with many of the same friends I hung out with during my
time of darkness. I wasn't necessarily indulging in the same sins
anymore, but I wasn't being sharpened either. These people were
the ones I had spent most of the previous five years with, and
they represented comfort to me. My experience has been that
comfort rarely, if ever, leads to growth. After a couple of months
of feeling stale and complacent, the realization hit me that I had
to become deliberate about cultivating relationships that would
challenge me spiritually. The truth was, I had a spiritual family
waiting on me at my church. I just had to trust God and let go
of the other one. After I made that decision, my life in Christ
absolutely took off.*

The idea of leaving a group of close friends behind is a difficult
one for most people to embrace. The Enemy uses this reluctance to
his advantage. Many rescued believers remain stuck in the ditch
of spiritual mediocrity—even after returning to the Lord—simply
because they cannot bring themselves to leave the relationships
of their sinful past. The Devil attempts to keep these prodigals
immobilized by repeatedly reminding them of two things:

1. *"It is unloving to break fellowship with your non-Christian
friends."*

2. *"Those Christians will never fully accept you."*

Both statements deal with very real feelings in the life of a
recovering believer. They are powerful.

And they are lies.

For a returning prodigal, breaking fellowship with unsaved
friends is not unloving. It is survival. There is an old proverb that
most of us learned from our grandparents:

"Birds of a feather flock together."

This wise saying simply states an undeniable principle: You will become like the people you spend the most time with. That is a fact of life. The Bible is chock-full of references to this truth, but perhaps the most straightforward of these is found in Second Corinthians:

"Do not be unequally yoked together with unbelievers. For what fellowship has righteousness with lawlessness? And what communion has light with darkness?" (2 Corinthians 6:14).

Christians are commanded not to "do life" primarily with non-Christians. This has nothing to do with being loving or unloving toward nonbelievers. It has everything to do with what hinders a believer from growing in Christ. How can someone inhabited by the Holy Spirit, recreated for a divine, eternal purpose, possibly be energized and lifted up by close fellowship with people who live from a completely worldly perspective? The answer to the question is obvious: As believers, we desperately need the company of others who love God and are called according to His purposes.

Invariably someone will say, "But I have a couple of unsaved friends that are like family to me. What about them?"

The necessity of cultivating a new family does not mean that we stop loving our unbelieving friends. In the case of some of these friends, it may not even mean breaking fellowship with them. If they really are like brothers or sisters to us, they will understand, accept, and respect our new life. If they are merely people with whom we have shared some sinful experiences, a break is most likely necessary. But regardless of which parts of the old family we may choose to retain, we must move consciously and intentionally toward the new.

Rich: About three years into my journey back to the Lord, I reached a crossroads. I was either going to pursue the life God made me for with every fiber of my being, or I was going to settle into a typical, mediocre American Christian existence. And I knew the only way I was going on with the Lord was if I began to get serious about developing some relationships in my life that would challenge and sharpen me as a man of God.

That was when I met a man named Scott Hurley. He was an attorney who taught a men's Sunday school class at his church. CH had known Scott for years and had asked him if he might be interested in leading a Bible study for guys at his home. Scott was all for the idea, and after the study had been going on for awhile, they invited me. I was a little reluctant at first; after all, I didn't even know this guy. But it didn't take long for me to give in, and I have to say, that fellowship of godly men was an agent of incredible spiritual growth in my life. Scott is a gifted, small-group facilitator with a unique insight into the Scriptures. But even more than the great truths we discussed, the sharpening effect of being in close fellowship with other godly men took me to the next level spiritually. There just is no substitute. We shared our hopes, dreams, fears, weaknesses, and hurts with each other. Barriers came down. We lifted each other up in prayer. I began to rediscover what a true spiritual family was. Although doing ministry has prevented me from going to the Bible study very often in recent years, I will forever be indebted to Scott and those guys for the role they played in my journey. The experience of fellowship at that Bible study group taught me that it was okay to let my guard down with other believers and helped prepare me to truly reconnect to my spiritual family at church.

Rich's experience is one of countless examples that prove what a house of cards Satan's second statement is. The Christians will accept you. But often it is up to us to make the first move. Rich could easily have been stubborn and refused to join the Bible study group or make the effort to embrace his church family again. It can sometimes be a challenging step, but if we will earnestly seek meaningful fellowship with a family of believers, God will provide those relationships. And when a Christian becomes a member of a strong spiritual family, his limitations begin to disappear.

And a glorious future begins to unfold.

A new hope

There are many pitfalls and difficulties that are inevitable when a believer walks away from the path God has marked out for him. But by far the most prevalent and debilitating is the loss of hope. A life lived apart from fellowship with Christ is a life that leads to hopelessness. But by the same token, when a wandering believer returns to the Lord, the rebirth of hope can be the greatest energizing force in his life.

Hope is the most precious commodity a Christian possesses. It is the single greatest difference between a Christ-follower and an unbeliever. Christians are people of hope in the midst of a hopeless world. The people of the world are starving for hope. When someone or something seems to offer a glimpse of it, people are drawn to it like a thirsty traveler to a desert oasis. One of the most often quoted verses from the Old Testament today talks about the hope God offers us:

" 'For I know the plans I have for you,' declares the Lord, 'plans to prosper you and not to harm you, plans to give you hope and a future' " (Jeremiah 29:11).

The words of this powerful verse have been claimed by many people in our culture, but it is only the born-again child of God who knows the true meaning and eternal nature of hope. Our hope and our future are in the Lord. He has created us, redeemed us, and set us apart for a divine purpose.

A purpose He knew long before we did.

Rich: I was aware by the time I was eighteen that God had called me to preach His Word. For three years, I fought the calling and began to pursue a secular degree just like everyone else my age. My ACT scores had qualified me for numerous scholarships. But I was still an immature mama's boy and wanted to live at home and attend the University of Tennessee. So for two and a half years, I became a commuter student without a major. Although I started off making very good grades at UT, it was only a matter of time before it hit me that I was nowhere close to pursuing the life God made me for.

Gradually, my interest in my studies faded, and my grades began to suffer until I had reached the brink of failing out of school. This would have been a colossal embarrassment to my family, most of whom expected me to pursue a medical career. So one day, sitting outside my history class, I told the Lord that I was done wasting my time on a secular liberal arts degree and that I was leaving school. I also told Him I was surrendering to the call to preach His Word. I went almost straight to my cousin Johnnie's house. He was my dad's age and had surrendered to the call to ministry many years before. He was hugely supportive and encouraging. I then told Rocky, my pastor. He, too, was incredibly supportive and helpful. Within a few months, he gave me my first opportunity to fill the pulpit in his absence. I won't lie; I was petrified. But as time went on, God kept giving me more opportunities to speak at different venues.

Obviously, as my life began to unravel spiritually, so did the expression of my gifts. I had dragged my feet about getting back in school so I could go to seminary. By about 1993, I was no longer preaching anymore. It was like the onslaught of sin in my life just choked out anything spiritual. When I began my journey back to God in 1997, I was virtually certain I had wasted too many opportunities to ever really be called on by God to use my gifts again.

But over the next several years, I began to discover that there was still a massive call on my life. In 2005, the Holy Spirit spoke to my heart about going into ministry for college students and young adults. This was a significant step for someone who had been passionate about youth ministry for nearly twenty years. Amazingly, in 2007, I had the privilege of coming on staff at my church as Director of College Ministry. It was a dream come true. I had done ministry off and on as a volunteer for twenty-one years, and now I was going to be on staff and actually get paid to do what I love.

But even after coming on board, I still had a dream I thought would never be realized. I was really unsure as to whether I would ever be asked to fill the pulpit in the main church service. To my amazement, my pastor asked me to fill in for him within just a few months. It was a watershed moment in my spiritual recovery. I knew Rocky was very protective and serious about who he allowed to teach in our church. Since that time, I have had the privilege of speaking for him on numerous occasions, and I have rediscovered my passionate belief that God created me primarily to communicate His truth through the spoken and written word. His calling on my life may have been sidetracked, delayed, and even mishandled, but I am convinced it has not been revoked. I am now more ready than ever to pursue it with all of my heart.

Rich learned firsthand a lesson a great many paralyzed believers would do well to embrace. The call they felt on their life years ago may have been hindered or even abandoned because of poor choices and circumstances, but if they are willing to step out in faith and believe God, He will restore the calling they once pursued as stewards of His kingdom.

It is a sad reality that many Christians remain immobilized to this day because of spiritual detours that left them wounded and under the delusion that they are no longer called according to God's purpose. But God is faithful. And while poor decisions can certainly rob us of specific opportunities, His callings do not go away. As the Bible makes clear:

"For God's gifts and His call are irrevocable" (Romans 11:29).

When broken believers return to Him in repentance, God offers them a new beginning, a new family, and a renewed calling. He offers them hope for a glorious future.

A future made even more glorious by the beautiful disaster of the past.

Questions to consider:

What steps do you need to take to move out of your spiritual comfort zone?

What specific people are you willing to break fellowship with for a time in order to pursue your God-given destiny?

Is there a specific family of believers you need to be intentional about cultivating fellowship with?

Truth to embrace:

The people we spend time with influence us profoundly.

"Do not be deceived: 'Evil company corrupts good habits' " (1 Corinthians 15:33 NKJV).

What we are willing to walk away from determines what God can do with us.

"Now the Lord had said to Abram: 'Get out of your country, From your family And from your father's house, To a land that I will show you' " (Genesis 12:1 NKJV).

We need a spiritual family to sharpen and encourage us.

"And let us consider how we may spur one another on toward love and good deeds, not giving up meeting together, as some are in the habit of doing, but encouraging one another—and all the more as you see the Day approaching" (Hebrews 10:24–25).

Chapter 13

Embracing the Wreckage

> "And we know that God causes all things to work together for good to those who love God, to those who are called according to His purpose" (Romans 8:28 NASB).

The disciples were speechless. They had seen Jesus do some pretty incredible things, but this topped them all. There must have been more than ten thousand people, counting the women and children, scattered across that hillside. And Jesus had fed every last one of them. With five loaves of bread and two small fish, the Master had fed the entire crowd. There were even twelve baskets of food left over.

One for each of them.

As the men loaded the boat with the food for the trip back across the Sea of Galilee, Jesus called to them.

"You guys go on ahead," said the Lord. "I'll meet you on the other side."

This brief conversation between Jesus and the twelve recorded in Matthew's gospel actually represents a microcosm of the Christian life. Like so many other elements of the believer's journey, it contains an instruction and a promise. Get in the boat. I'll meet you on the other side.

What Jesus did not tell the disciples that day was the same thing many Christians are also woefully unaware of. Bound up in that promise of getting to the other side was something they didn't see coming.

A storm.

"The boat was already a considerable distance from land, buffeted by the waves because the wind was against it" (Matthew 14:24).

Rich: As a young believer, I had many hopes and dreams about what my life as a Christ follower would look like in the years ahead. I think all young Christians envision their future to one extent or another. I saw myself with a family, a nice home, and a modest income from doing the Lord's work. I wouldn't say that I necessarily saw myself being the senior pastor of a church, but I definitely had aspirations of speaking to large numbers of people. But what I never saw was the horrific turn my life would take in my late twenties. I didn't see that one coming. Not in a million years. When I was young, you could have never convinced me that any of that stuff would be part of the journey. Certainly not if the journey was going to amount to anything. It never occurred to me that God could use the depths of my darkness to take me to heights I never dreamed possible. That just doesn't make sense.

The unbreakable promise

Every person that ever comes to Christ is given a promise. Actually, they are offered many, but there is one that is an absolute certainty: God will finish what He started. Throughout church history, many have debated the specificity of this point. But Rich, Wes, and the apostle Paul are certainly convinced.

"And I am certain that God, who began the good work within you, will continue his work until it is finally finished on the day when Christ Jesus returns" (Philippians 1:6 NLT).

In this verse, Paul references one of the most powerful truths associated with the Christian life: If God begins a work in you, He will finish it. The implications of such a statement are far-reaching yet intensely personal. But as awesome as its message is for believers, there is much Philippians 1:6 does not tell us. Like what happens between the beginning and the completion.

Because that can be just about anything.

Wes: When I was eighteen, you could have placed a script of the next five years of my life in front of me, and I would have laughed in your face. I knew how my life was going to go. I was going to walk with God through college, help disciple middle school and high school kids, meet a beautiful, godly Christian girl, get married, have kids, and live happily ever after. I would have never believed the disastrous direction I chose could ever be part of a godly man's life. Those kinds of things just can't be part of the story for true servants of God.

Actually they can. Let us take a random sample of Bible heroes from the book of Genesis. Abraham had sex with his wife's handmaiden in direct disobedience to God. Isaac lied about Rebekah being his wife, putting her in great danger to save his own skin. Jacob swindled his brother out of his birthright and then deceived his blind, aging father to seal the deal.

Surely such seedy characters could never be named among the choicest of God's servants. Yet in the book of Exodus, when God reveals Himself to the man who would define much of Old Testament history, the Lord gives the following introduction:

> When the Lord saw Moses coming to take a closer look, God called to him from the middle of the bush, "Moses! Moses!"

"Here I am!" Moses replied.

> "Do not come any closer," the Lord warned. "Take off your sandals, for you are standing on holy ground. I am the God of your father—the God of Abraham, the God of Isaac, and the God of Jacob" (Exodus 2:4–6 NLT).

The implications of God's announcement of Himself to Moses are astounding:

"Hello, Moses. I am the God of an adulterer, a liar, and a swindler."

He would also be the God of a murderer. One who had spent the past forty years hiding from his infamous crime on the backside of a wasteland. But God was about to reveal to Moses something He desperately wants every child of His to know: He means to finish what He started.

Even if what's left is a train wreck.

The inexplicable explanation

God wants to finish what He started. That is the message of this book. It is the message to the guy reading this page right now who cannot imagine how a holy God could possibly work with the sexual carnage of his life. It is the message to the young Christian woman who wonders how she could ever live the life she was made for with two kids and no husband. It is the message to everyone whose spiritual life has been characterized more by failure than fruit; more by wreckage than results.

You are not alone, child of God. You qualify for the promise in Philippians 1:6. But like so many other believers, you have discovered that something happens between the beginning and ending of the verse. Something between God starting a work in you and God finishing that work.

Something called life.

The great news is that there is an explanation for the white spaces in Philippians 1:6. God would not give us such a powerful promise without such an explanation. He not only finishes what He starts, He works with the wreckage in between. The same man through whom God penned the promise of Philippians 1:6 also was given the privilege of writing God's profoundly amazing explanation. It is not only the theme verse of this chapter, but a precious treasure to every person who has ever believed God to somehow make sense of their train wreck. The New Living Translation renders it as follows:

"And we know that God causes everything to work together for the good of those who love God and are called according to his purpose for them" (Romans 8:28).

It may be the single greatest verse about the Christian life in the entire Bible. If you belong to Him, God causes all things to work together for your good. All things? Yes, all things.

All good things?

No. All things.

Mistakes? Yes.

Tragedies? You bet.

Bible study? Of course.

Prayer? Definitely.

Heartbreak? Sure.

Sin? Absolutely.

On the surface, it seems impossible, if not almost blasphemous, that a bunch of junk could work together for good in a believer's life. But it can. Because of a little Greek word in the middle of the verse, sunergeo, which is translated "work together." It is the word from which we get our English word synergy. It refers to individual components working in tandem to create a greater force than that of the components themselves. It makes sense in theory.

But not in life.

How can drug abuse and a pornography addiction and financial disaster and a DUI and a child out of wedlock possibly create synergy? That's a very fair question. And here is the awe-inspiring answer: They can't—but God causes them to!

That is the inexplicable explanation of Romans 8:28! Our awesome, indescribable God can cause the most painful, ugly, heartbreaking, filthy things to work together in the life of a believer and somehow produce—get this—good. We all have train wrecks. And we have a God who wants to make the wreckage embraceable.

No matter how tangled it may be.

Wes: I know God has given me a powerful testimony since He brought me back into fellowship with Him. He has already allowed it to impact lives and has used me more than I ever thought He could. But as wonderful as my return to the Lord has been, my life is not a neatly packaged story tied up with a ribbon. The spring after I returned to the Lord, my girlfriend and I decided to give our relationship one more chance. It seemed the right thing to do, especially since we had a child together. But after a few months, it became apparent that the relationship was not healthy. It was dragging us down spiritually and causing us both to struggle in our walks with God. In July of that year, we decided to break up. I do not mean to imply that she was the problem. I am confident she was trying her best to follow the Lord as I was. But I grew more spiritually in that next month than I ever had in my life. I felt like I was finally free to pursue the life God made me for.

Then I got the call. I was going to be a father again. It was like being kicked in the gut a thousand times. I can only imagine what she was feeling. For me, it felt like everything I had done, all the progress I had made since coming back to fellowship with Christ, was meaningless. I was so angry at myself for letting God, her and everyone else down. The Devil's assault was relentless. "You've really blown it now. God will never use you again. You might as well give up." For a fleeting moment, I just wanted to quit. But strangely, his attacks didn't have traction this time. The harder the Enemy tried to undo all that God had done in my life, the more the Holy Spirit rose up within me and strengthened my resolve to stay the course. I refused to grant the Devil a foothold.

There were many battles to fight. There was the question of what to do about a relationship I had been certain I was supposed to end. A lot of well-meaning people didn't understand why we didn't just get married and make the best of it. But at the time I just did not feel at peace about pursuing marriage. I told her I would be there to help raise both our kids, even if we weren't going to be together as a couple. Having my two beautiful boys has been a blessing from God, even though the situation is much more complicated for them than I ever intended or envisioned. The second pregnancy was such a bizarre twist to my story that I was even hesitant about sharing it in this book. But as I sought the Holy Spirit's guidance, God spoke to my heart and made me realize that it's all part of my train wreck. For the first time in a long time, I have learned to genuinely trust in the power of the Holy Spirit to live a pure and holy life as a young adult. I know now that I have to share my story in order to give hope to people whose wreckage is every bit as tangled as mine. I am doing my best one day at a time to embrace it. And I know in my heart that God is using it. I want people to know that God can bring grace to their train wreck, too.

The beautiful disaster

Grace seldom makes sense. Why would a holy, righteous God decide to use such irresponsible and self-indulgent behavior to work together for good in a person's life? For believers, the answer to that question is right there in Romans 8:28: Because they are called according to His purposes. Yet such an expression of grace is still almost beyond our comprehension.

Why would God look at a person with so much promise and opportunity as Rich had as a young man and not immediately cast him aside after he selfishly threw it all down the drain? Why would God continue to use the testimony of someone like Wes, even after he had the audacity and carelessness to bring a second child into the world out of wedlock? The answers to questions like these may never be known or understood. But we do know a couple of things: God is a fanatic about finishing what He starts.

And He also had a book to write.

We didn't write this book for people who claim to have it all together. We didn't even write it for people who have recovered from past mistakes and failures. We wrote it to give people hope in the midst of their disasters. Their born-again-Christian disasters. It's for the husband, father, and community group leader who is devastated with guilt over the affair he had with someone in the church. It's for the single Christian girl who goes from relationship to relationship and gives herself away to every guy she dates. It is for the young adult believer locked in feverish battle with a spirit of homosexuality.

With all of His divine heart, God wants to take the nightmare of your life and turn it into a dream again. He isn't interested in fairy tales or neatly packaged anecdotes from a Christian magazine. Just real people with real stories.

Twisted, mangled wreckage that God wants to turn into a beautiful disaster.

Rich: At forty-six years old, I have learned to embrace the wreckage of my past for what it is: a testimony. Certainly there are lasting consequences to the sins and failures of my former life. One of those is the lack of a college degree. Even before my train jumped the tracks, there was a huge lack of maturity and responsibility lurking beneath the surface of my life. Despite my highly touted credentials coming out of high school, I never finished college. Yet God has blessed me financially and has actually allowed me to use my high school education to disciple college students!

Another lingering effect of my dark years is my singleness. My irresponsible lifestyle, and particularly the pornography addiction, precluded my pursuing healthy relationships with the opposite sex during a very crucial time in my life. While I would never limit God as to what He might do in the future, I have learned to accept and celebrate my singleness as a unique and effective position from which to do ministry. I am able to devote a great deal of my time to the study of God's Word and preparation to speak. As a college pastor, my availability to my students is far greater than it would be if I had a family of my own. It has also given me a deep appreciation for the family of God and the brothers and sisters in Christ I have in my life. They are truly my family. I often tell people I am the least lonely single person I know. God certainly gets all the glory and praise for that.

Embracing the wreckage of one's life is absolutely essential to moving into the place God wants each of us to be. We cannot effectively move toward the glorious future He has prepared for us until we learn to celebrate the beautiful disaster of our past.

And there is no time for celebration quite like the present.

Questions to consider:

Are you willing to trust God to use all the circumstances of your life for your good and His glory?

Are you willing to turn your train wreck over to God before you finish the last chapter?

Truth to embrace:

We often see God's plan only in the rearview mirror.

"Then Joseph said to his brothers, 'Come close to me.' When they had done so, he said, 'I am your brother Joseph, the one you sold into Egypt! And now, do not be distressed and do not be angry with yourselves for selling me here, because it was to save lives that God sent me ahead of you' " (Genesis 45:4–5).

What the Enemy intends for evil, God can use for good.

"Joseph said to them, 'Do not be afraid, for am I in the place of God? But as for you, you meant evil against me; but God meant it for good, in order to bring it about as it is this day'"(Genesis 50:19-20 NKJV).

Even the parts of our story we regret can be used by God for His glory.

"But whatever were gains to me I now consider loss for the sake of Christ" (Philippians 3:7).

Chapter 14

No Day but Today

Every believer has a glorious future. Regardless of how heinous the
sins of your past may be, no matter how bleak the circumstances
of your life may look, God has plans to give you a future. And the
purpose of this last chapter is to make you aware of a revolutionary
truth about that future:

It's not what you think it is.

The day that never came

*Rich: Even when I was walking through my dark years, there
were moments when I thought about my faith. I think I actually
convinced myself that I would still arrive at the future God
desired for my life. But it wasn't a present reality to me. I would
have thoughts like, "Someday I'll get back into ministry again,"
or "Someday I'll have victory over these sin habits in my life."*

> *And then the most common, "Someday I'll get my life straight with the Lord." It was not until God brought me back into the light that I realized how misguided those statements were.*

Misguided indeed. Yet well-meaning Christians make such statements and entertain such thoughts all the time. "Someday" they'll give everything to Christ. "Someday," when they get through college. "Someday," when they meet their future spouse. "Someday," when they get married. "Someday," when they have kids. "Someday," when their kids are grown. The list is exhaustive, running the gamut of noble Christian aspirations. There is only one problem:

"Someday" never comes.

This is the inevitable quandary for a person who sees his future in Christ in a "someday" context. It is the often fatal mistake made by many who may genuinely desire a dynamic walk with Christ. They think their future is "someday." But they are wrong.

You can't do anything someday. Anything you aspire to do someday will never be done. Because someday does not really exist. Don't believe it? Try this experiment.

Find someone of the opposite sex you might like to go out with (your spouse would be a wise choice, if you're married). Muster up the courage to call them, and make a date. Tell them you'll pick them up at 7:30 someday. Let us know how your date goes.

Someday is a figment of our well-intentioned imaginations. It is a safe time and place for scheduling some of our most challenging tasks because it always seems to be "out there somewhere." But the beautiful reality every child of God needs to embrace is that someday does indeed eventually arrive. It's just that no one notices. Because when it gets here, we don't call it "someday." We call it by the name of the only time we can ever do anything:

We call it "today."

Our glorious present

There is only one time when a person can truly surrender his life to the lordship of Christ. There is only one time when a wounded believer can return to the cross for healing and restoration. There is only one time for repentance; only one time when we can get it right. The Bible makes it abundantly clear what that time is:

"For God says, 'At just the right time, I heard you. On the day of salvation, I helped you.

Indeed, the "right time" is now. Today is the day of salvation'" (2 Corinthians 6:2 NLT).

The right time is now. God could not make it any plainer. For the pornography addict reading this page, the time is now. Put the book down, get on your knees, and ask the Father to set you on the road to recovery. For the drug abuser, put the book down. The time is now. Trust God today for the deliverance He is more than able to accomplish. For the cheating spouse, put the book down. The time is now. Call the other person, and end it today. Then ask your heavenly Father to engulf your life in His sea of limitless grace. For every broken believer reading these words:

Put the book down.

Hit your knees.

The time is now.

Today is your day of salvation.

Rich: One of the things my journey to the dark and back has taught me is that we simply are not guaranteed tomorrow. Over the past several years, God has been revealing this truth to me even more powerfully. Christ did not die for us so that we could sit back in our recliners and watch ESPN until He returns. We must develop a carpe diem faith that seizes every day as a precious moment God has given us to live radically for Him in the present. This perspective has enabled me to seek His truth more passionately, preach His Word more powerfully and love His people more boldly.

So intent was Jesus on proclaiming this present tense quality of our faith that He once had the temerity to approach a Samaritan woman in public. Flying directly in the face of intense social prejudice, Jesus, a Jewish man, walked up to a well and asked a Samaritan woman for a drink. In the conversation that followed, it became clear that the Lord was not only crossing a sacred cultural barrier but a religious one as well. This woman was not only a Samaritan.

She was a moral catastrophe.

In the fourth chapter of John's gospel, this watershed moment in history is recorded.

> "Go and get your husband," Jesus told her.
>
> "I don't have a husband," the woman replied.
>
> Jesus said, "You're right! You don't have a husband—for you have had five husbands, and you aren't even married to the man you're living with now. You certainly spoke the truth!" (John 4:16–18 NLT).

The manner in which Jesus addressed this woman may seem blunt and uncaring at first glance. But in the dialogue that followed, the Lord exposed the reality of her life with a compassion the likes of which she had never experienced.

Like so many in our culture, this woman was religious. Yes, she was five-times married and currently shacking up with a man. But as her question to Jesus revealed, she was also a worshipper of God.

"So tell me, why is it that you Jews insist that Jerusalem is the only place of worship, while we Samaritans claim it is here at Mount Gerizim, where our ancestors worshipped?" (John 4:20 NLT).

This immoral, adulterous Samaritan woman had a spiritual heritage. She had religion. And as the conversation continued, she even told Jesus she had a faith. A belief that everything in her train wreck would make sense. Someday.

"The woman said, 'I know the Messiah is coming—the one who is called Christ. When he comes, he will explain everything to us' " (John 4:25 NLT).

Jesus knew this woman's problem. It was not her past, though it was littered with bad decisions. It was not her future, though it must have looked discouraging given the circumstances of her life. Her problem was that she lived her life looking for something to happen "someday." A Messiah who would "someday" come and finally give meaning to the disaster of her life. It was a someday she longed for. And she didn't even realize it was staring her in the face.

"Jesus said to her, 'I who speak to you am He' " (John 4:26 NKJV).

Suddenly, in an instant, this woman's past, present, and future were revolutionized! The Messiah she dreamed would come someday was here! She was face to face with the Son of God. There was no more waiting. At that moment, her future became her present. Her "someday" became her today.

Wes: During the five years or so that I lived away from the Lord, there were several times when I took brief glances back toward the narrow path. But that's just what they were— glances. None of those momentary changes in direction ever "stuck." I always ended up sinking right back into my life of sin. I know now it was because of my unwillingness to give God everything and lay my life completely at the foot of His cross. There was also all kinds of doubt on my part as to whether I could ever be part of God's kingdom again. Don't get me wrong—in the back of my mind, I hoped it might happen, but it seemed like something that would have to come way down the road. You know—"someday." It wasn't until the fall of 2009 that I realized "someday" had to be today. That Thanksgiving weekend, I just knew it was now or never. There were no more "somedays." It was "go time." Thank God, Jesus was true to His Word. That particular "today" really was the day of salvation.

It was the day my journey back to freedom began. I still have a lot of issues to deal with in my life, but every day I wake up with a renewed hope that they are not just my issues. They are God's issues, and every new today is a step toward the future that I am believing Him for.

The only faith that works

James was a straightforward guy. The brother of Jesus, who wrote the little epistle that has become one of the most beloved books of the Bible, didn't mince words when he talked about faith.

"Even so faith, if it has no works, is dead" (James 2:17 NASB).

A modern-day, blue-collar translation of this theology might sound something like this: "If your faith ain't workin', it ain't real."

Faith is the single most important element to living the Christian life. Nothing else is a close second. You might say that faith is the practical vehicle by which all the theological benefits of knowing Christ come to the believer. The writer of Hebrews certainly thought of faith on such a level. At one point, he even gave us perhaps the only definition of biblical faith found anywhere in Scripture. And it is one we need to take particular notice of.

"Now faith is the substance of things hoped for, the evidence of things not seen" (Hebrews 11:1 KJV).

Here in the eleventh chapter of Hebrews, this anonymous writer penned a powerful definition of a powerful word. Bible scholars have used this verse for centuries, both to define faith as well as to point out its various components.

Certain words grab our attention as we read the passage. Powerful words like "substance" and "hoped" and "evidence." Those are all expressions of the depth and majesty of the thing that pleases God most. But if we aren't careful, we will miss something when we read Hebrews 11:1. We will miss the most important word in the verse.

And the most important characteristic of faith.

In virtually every translation of the Bible, the eleventh chapter of Hebrews, the greatest chapter on faith in all Scripture, begins not with the word "faith," but with the word "now." This is not merely a linguistic expression. This is a description of the only kind of faith that can ever work for a child of God:

Present-tense faith.

This is the type of faith that is far more than mere words or statements of belief. It is more than an imaginary ticket to heaven. This is the faith that is able to lift broken, wounded believers out of the pit of despair, out of the pigpen, and carry them back to the Father's house. This is the faith you must embrace.

Do you need to believe God to forgive your past? Believe Him now. Do you need to declare your faith that Christ can heal the wounds of your failures? Declare it now. Do you need to ask in faith for God to restore you to fellowship with Him as His precious son or daughter? Ask now. Present-tense faith is the only kind of faith that ever makes a difference. It touches the heart of God. It topples giants. It moves mountains.

Not just any faith.

Now faith.

Make it count

This book was written for broken believers; those paralyzed by the guilt and shame of failure experienced after the point of their salvation. Many of you were paralyzed when you picked up this book.

But you picked it up.

Now the time has come to put it down. The almighty God of eternity past and eternity future is standing right now in your present moment, waiting for your next move. This isn't the time for fleeting glances in His direction. This isn't a move to put off until "someday" comes.

It's "go time."

Your Father is waiting. He has been waiting all along. He has plans for you. Good plans to enable you to embrace your wreckage and to give you a glorious future. Your long nightmare is coming to an end. Your "someday" is today.

Now put the book down.

And make today count.

Questions to consider:

Is your faith more focused on your past, your future, or your present?

Are you ready to put this book down and run into the arms of your heavenly Father?

Truth to embrace:

There is no time like the present to return to the Lord.

"As has just been said: 'Today, if you hear his voice, do not harden your hearts as you did in the rebellion' " (Hebrews 3:15).

God is always calling His wayward children home.

"The Spirit and the bride say, 'Come!' And let the one who hears say, 'Come!' Let the one who is thirsty come; and let the one who wishes take the free gift of the water of life" (Revelation 22:17).

God desires our repentance even more than we desire to give it.

"So he got up and went to his father. But while he was still a long way off, his father saw him and was filled with compassion for him; he ran to his son, threw his arms around him and kissed him" (Luke 15:20).

Epilogue

April 24, 2011
Easter Sunday

It is difficult to put into words how gloriously the grace of God has transformed my life over the past fourteen years. My dark journey came to an end in 1997. But learning to walk in the light again was anything but instantaneous. It has been, and continues to be, a journey marked by many hills and valleys; by majestic mountain vistas and sometimes dark, lonely tunnels.

But through it all, the faithfulness of God has been overwhelming. He has rescued, restored, and transformed the life of this once broken believer. Fourteen years ago, I took the hand of Christ and He pulled me out of the pit. I was thirty-three years old and owned virtually nothing save for a few possessions in a rented basement apartment. I was staring at a mountain of debt I never thought possible to overcome. Yet God's supernatural provision has been so great in my life that I was debt-free within five years, and in 2008, He allowed me to build my dream home. It is now a place of healing, restoration, and spiritual sanctuary where God's Spirit continues to transform lives.

When I came back to the Lord in 1997, I had not preached a sermon in over five years. I doubted I would ever get the opportunity to use my speaking gift to any consequence again. But in 2005, the Lord called me into college ministry, and in January of 2007, I was brought on staff by my church. God has given me the honor of being a pastor and teacher to an incredible group of students. I now speak weekly to a gathering of these young adults and even have the unbelievable privilege of filling the pulpit when our senior pastor is away. I believe with all my heart that God is calling me to use the rest of my life to communicate His truth through the spoken and written word.

As for Wes, the transformation in his life over the past seventeen months has been like nothing I have ever observed in all my years of walking with God. The depth of darkness he was living in less than two years ago has been radically replaced by the glorious light of fellowship with Christ. His testimony is affecting students and young adults in a powerful way through ministry as well as through simple conversation.

Wes is the father of two healthy boys. Although God's grace has been evident throughout the journey, it is by no means an ideal scenario. Life seldom is. But Wes is trusting God every day for the wisdom and opportunity to bring up his sons in the fear and admonition of the Lord. As further testimony to the amazing grace of our Savior, the boys' mom is now a follower of Christ.

Neither of us knows for sure where God's grace will direct our journeys next. But we do know that today, perhaps better than we have ever known before, He has a wonderful and glorious plan for our lives. We know beyond a shadow of a doubt that one day in the presence of our God is better than a thousand days without Him. He has turned our mourning into dancing. He has restored our brokenness. He has withheld nothing from us that would bring us peace, fulfillment, and joy. We can claim with confidence the words of Psalm 84:

"Better is one day in your courts than a thousand elsewhere; I would rather be a doorkeeper in the house of my God than dwell in the tents of the wicked. For the Lord God is a sun and shield; the

Lord bestows favor and honor; no good thing does he withhold from those whose walk is blameless" (Psalm 84:10–11 NIV).

No good thing does God withhold. That is the story of these two doorkeepers.

We both pray that it becomes yours.

Rich Beeler

Notes

Chapter 9

1. Taken from Life Today, a television program hosted by James Robison. (No permission required)

Chapter 11

1. Toplady, Augustus M., "Rock of Ages," 1776. (Public domain)